STOP

Don't Plan a
Wedding
Without This Book

Laura Weatherly

ALPHA
A member of Penguin Group (USA) Inc.

This book is dedicated to all my friends in the D.C. wedding industry who have made this job so entertaining! You know who you are, and I couldn't have done it for so many years without you!

ALPHA BOOKS

Published by the Penguin Group

Penguin Group (USA) Inc., 375 Hudson Street, New York, New York 10014, U.S.A.

Penguin Group (Canada), 10 Alcorn Avenue, Toronto, Ontario, Canada M4V 3B2 (a division of Pearson Penguin Canada Inc.)

Penguin Books Ltd, 80 Strand, London WC2R 0RL, England

Penguin Ireland, 25 St Stephen's Green, Dublin 2, Ireland (a division of Penguin Books Ltd)

Penguin Group (Australia), 250 Camberwell Road, Camberwell, Victoria 3124, Australia (a division of Pearson Australia Group Pty Ltd)

Penguin Books India Pvt Ltd, 11 Community Centre, Panchsheel Park, New Delhi—110 017, India

Penguin Group (NZ), cnr Airborne and Rosedale Roads, Albany, Auckland 1310, New Zealand (a division of Pearson New Zealand Ltd)

Penguin Books (South Africa) (Pty) Ltd, 24 Sturdee Avenue, Rosebank, Johannesburg 2196, South Africa

Penguin Books Ltd, Registered Offices: 80 Strand, London WC2R 0RL, England

International Standard Book Number: 1-59257-445-9
Library of Congress Catalog Card Number: 2005932773

08 07 06 05   8 7 6 5 4 3 2 1

Interpretation of the printing code: The rightmost number of the first series of numbers is the year of the book's printing; the rightmost number of the second series of numbers is the number of the book's printing. For example, a printing code of 05-1 shows that the first printing occurred in 2005.

Printed in the United States of America

Publisher: *Marie Butler-Knight*
Editorial Director: *Mike Sanders*
Senior Managing Editor: *Jennifer Bowles*
Senior Acquisitions Editor: *Paul Dinas*
Development Editor: *Christy Wagner*
Production Editor: *Megan Douglass*

Copy Editor: *Emily Bell*
Cover/Book Designer: *Rebecca Harmon*
Indexer: *Angie Bess*
Layout: *Rebecca Harmon*
Proofreading: *John Etchison*

Contents

Contents

Contents

Contents

Introduction

Sure, your wedding is a big deal—perhaps one of the most important days of your life. You've found your soul mate, and you want to celebrate with 200 of your nearest and dearest friends and family members. It's understandable that you'd want this day to be as close to perfect as possible, but a wedding should not make you break out in hives, want to change your name and leave the country, or have a complete meltdown over what type of veil to wear. And most important, keep in mind that weddings are *never* perfect.

Once you get used to the idea that your wedding will not be absolutely perfect, you'll be a much happier bride (and much easier to live and work with). Weddings are complex events involving lots of people and, therefore, can never be absolutely flawless. No matter how carefully you plan, something will go not precisely as you intended. The good news is that if you've planned properly, you'll almost never even notice one or two tiny blips. However, if you have forgotten some major elements or made some bad bridal decisions early on, you may have more bad memories of your wedding day than happy ones.

Not to worry, though. I'm here to walk you through the planning process and point out the warning signs and potential pitfalls along the way. I tell you who to hire and who to avoid, what tricks not to fall for, and how to work with the people you do hire so you get the best service possible. This is not a girlie bridal book with pretty pictures of bridal bouquets. There are plenty of those on bookstore shelves already. This is a guerrilla wedding planning guide for brides who are serious about doing it right—and staying sane in the process.

Planning a wedding should be fun, or at the very least, shouldn't make you lose your mind. More than knowing what you should do when you plan an event this complex and emotional, you need to know what you *shouldn't* do. Most brides end up with wedding disaster stories because of things they did incorrectly from the beginning. Before you start bringing home bridal magazines so heavy they could be used as doorstops and making a list of the 101 things you must do before you can say "I do," take a deep breath and settle in for some no-holds-barred, insider wedding planning advice straight from the trenches. This is the type of advice your mother would never give you and your girlfriends just don't know. It's the real deal from a wedding planner who's seen it all, knows what works and what doesn't, and is going to let you in on all the secrets.

Sure, you may have friends who have gotten married and are eager to share their newfound expertise, but beware! No bride can be truly objective about her wedding (this goes along the same lines as every mother thinking her baby is beautiful). Although your best friend may assure you that her cousin's all-'70s cover band did a great job at her wedding, proceed with caution. Getting advice from friends can be a lifesaver, but don't take advice blindly. Remember that recent brides have only slightly more experience than you do.

Your mother may be equally excited to share her wedding knowledge with you, but you'll find that weddings have come a long way from the punch-and-cake receptions of the past. What was once a relatively simple task has now become a planning feat of such precision and detail that it would make military generals weep. As a matter of fact, I've seen plenty of powerful career women reduced to tears when faced with the sheer scope of planning a wedding (or the prospect of choosing table linens). So be gracious about your mother's advice, but keep this book close at hand.

Not that this book intends to take the place of your mother's free-flowing advice or those merciless checklists found in every wedding magazine published. On the contrary. This is simply your first line of defense before delving into the world of wedding planning. This book teaches you what not to do before you rush out and start madly planning and make some serious wedding goofs.

Introduction

This is the down-and-dirty, behind-the-scenes advice that will help you avoid common wedding planning mistakes and silence that little voice that keeps telling you that you should have eloped. You'll get the lowdown on everything from finding the perfect reception site to how not to morph into Bridezilla. What you won't find are lists of flowers and their special meanings, ways to incorporate Navajo traditions into your ceremony, or how to painstakingly make your own origami favors. To be honest, I think making your own origami favors is a horrible idea, and I have the paper cuts to back it up.

Everything you'll find in this book is realistic and road-tested over hundreds of weddings. I let you in on the things wedding planners talk about when we get together and compare notes (and no, we don't talk about the trendiest shades of pink and the latest look in chair covers). What we do talk about is the nitty-gritty of wedding planning and what planning mistakes brides bring to us to fix—to put it simply, what works and what doesn't. You're going to get some tested wedding planner secrets, plus learn what things to worry about and what not to stress over. You might be surprised at the things wedding professionals worry about and the things we know just don't matter as much.

Wedding planning should be as individual as each bride, and there is definitely no one-size-fits-all approach here. Start at the beginning, or jump around as you need to. This book is all about customizing your wedding and your wedding planning so it actually works for you, not for some mythical bride with all the time in the world and an endless budget. I give you permission to secretly hate those brides.

So sit back and get ready for a whole new kind of wedding advice told just like your best friend would tell you (if she'd planned a few hundred weddings and lived to tell the tale). Finally, the book that every wedding planner secretly wishes her clients would read and every bride will be thankful she did!

Acknowledgments

Thanks to my agent, Peter Rubie, who always finds great opportunities for me, and my acquisitions editor, Paul Dinas, who made the process so much easier. A big thanks to Megan Douglass, Christy Wagner, and Emily Bell for their editing and input. I have to thank my friends in the wedding industry for their help and expertise in writing this book: Juan Carlos Briceno (who also happens to be my husband and a fabulously talented photographer), Jenny Lehman, Ric Marino, Anne Dutton, Michelle Alberg, Nick Perez, Monte Durham, Christine Cadima, and Sarah Gallo. Thanks to James and Liz for sharing their favorite travel spots. Special thanks to my wonderful husband for his constant support while I juggled writing, book tours, and planning weddings. Finally, thanks to the many brides who have let me be a part of their beautiful weddings.

1

First Things First: How to Plan a Wedding Without Wanting to Elope

Congratulations! You've probably just gotten engaged and are still on the emotional high that caused you to call every girlfriend the moment after your darling fiancé slipped the ring on your finger. You may have already started a collection of bridal magazines so thick they rival the phone book and begun brainstorming with your mother or best friend about the absolute perfect shade of burgundy for the bridesmaids' dresses.

Stop right there. One of the biggest mistakes brides make is getting caught up in the initial engagement frenzy and making decisions too quickly. In this chapter, I tell you how to start your wedding planning the right way before things get out of control and your sanity is unsalvageable. You'll learn how to prioritize and compromise, as well as how to keep your friends and family happy without making yourself miserable. So drop that bridal magazine and listen up!

Taking Charge Before It Gets Out of Control

For some unknown reason, when people see an engagement ring on your finger, they feel compelled to share every detail of their wedding and dispense lots of dubious advice. Don't panic when people ask you about wedding-related things that haven't even occurred to you yet.

Remember, this is *your* wedding, and just because your co-worker had her entire wedding planned the week after she got engaged (a doubtful story, anyway) doesn't mean you need to rush out and start planning yours in a frenzy. Let's look at a few easy steps you can take to stay in control of your planning from the start.

The Best Time

One of the very first decisions you have to make is when to get married. Almost the second you announce your engagement, people will ask you "When's the big day?" Depending on where you live and your lifestyle, various factors will influence your decision.

Considerations When Setting a Wedding Date

O What times of the year have the nicest weather where you live?

O Will any major events in town, such as college graduations or conventions, conflict with your wedding and cause you to compete for hotel rooms?

O If you have lots of friends or family with children, will the wedding conflict with their school schedules?

O If you select a holiday or long weekend, will your guests already have plans or family obligations?

O What's your schedule like? If you're a teacher, for instance, scheduling around a break or holiday can give you extra days off. I've had lawyers even have to reschedule their wedding date to avoid a big trial!

Once you have run potential wedding dates by your families and come up with a perfect time of year or a handful of potential dates, be sure to tell your nearest and dearest. Then stick with it! If you keep changing your date, you'll invariably lose people who just can't keep up with the changes or have made other plans.

Nip It in the Bud

In the joy surrounding your engagement, it is easy to feel like you would love each and every person you've ever met to be at your wedding. You'll be getting lots of congratulations from oodles of people, from the co-worker who you only say hello to in the hallway to the friend of a friend you only see at occasional parties. This is a good thing, right?

Now here's the hard part: you must fight the urge to invite people to the wedding. Any people. "Piece of cake," you say. "We haven't even made the guest list." Let me tell you, *not* inviting people is easier said than done.

DO Handle People Politely

There are a few ways to deal with people inviting themselves to your wedding or assuming they're invited. First of all, never issue a verbal invitation or say anything that would lead anyone to think you're inviting them. If they persist, you can say very politely that you and your fiancé haven't made any decisions as to the size of the wedding. When you're further along in your planning, it is reasonable to tell people that due to the size restraints of your church or reception site, you have unfortunately had to limit the number of guests.

It never fails: the very people who would never cross your mind as potential wedding guests will be the ones who assume they're invited and tell you how excited they are about your wedding. This puts you in an awkward position, but remember you aren't the one who is making a social blunder.

Be sure to tell your fiancé not to run out and start inviting the world as well. I've known many grooms who casually invited everyone at their favorite sports bar only to find themselves in serious hot water with their bride-to-be. You and your fiancé being on the same page from the beginning will save lots of arguments later.

Your Fiancé Wants *What?*

As perfectly matched as you and your intended are, inevitably, the two of you will have differing ideas on one or two (or more) elements of your wedding. Or maybe you don't agree on anything having to do with the wedding! He wants a DJ, and you want a swing band. You prefer a seated dinner, and he insists on a buffet. He wants the wedding to have a Bruce Springsteen theme, and you'd rather die a thousand deaths.

To survive the next few months so you actually make it to the altar, you'll have to learn the art of compromise. Here are a few tips I've learned over my years of counseling brides.

Ways to Make Everyone Happy (Including You!)

○ Determine how important an issue is to you. Remember that if you go to the mat for this one, you might not have any negotiating power when something really important comes up later.

○ Is there an easy compromise so everyone will be happy? For example, having a band for half the reception and a DJ for the rest is a great compromise.

○ How important is this to your fiancé? If he's a shutterbug, delegating the choice of photographer is a great way to get him involved and help him feel included.

○ Will this one issue change your overall wedding, or is it pretty minor?

Often you can make all the players happy without any one person making tons of sacrifices. I've had brides who were in a stand-off over whether to have a seated dinner versus a buffet, and the solution turned out to be serving the first course at the table and then having guests go to a buffet. Or we've had the first two courses served and had a lavish dessert buffet. There's always a way to compromise, and if you learn this early on, you will have a much happier and stress-free engagement!

DON'T Try to Always Get Your Way

Despite every bridal magazine telling you it's *your* day, remember it's not a day to run roughshod over everyone else (including your husband-to-be). The way you treat people during your engagement, from your future in-laws to your mother, will be remembered for a long time. Before you decide to take a stand and tell your future mother-in-law that you hate the place she's chosen for a rehearsal dinner, think long and hard. There is a price to pay for always getting your way!

Keeping Your Families from Driving You Insane

Now that you've learned to compromise, you have to learn to balance the input of both your families. You might be used to your parents' opinions, but keep in mind that you have a whole other side of the family to take into consideration—his.

The best way to keep both families as happy as clams is to communicate up front and be completely fair. Problems arise when one side of the family invites three times the number of guests as the other side just because they didn't know their guest limit.

Ground Rules for Dealing With Families

○ Facilitate a meeting between the parents, if they haven't already met. It is nice if the groom's parents make the call to the bride's family.

○ Tell both families the size and style of wedding you intend to have.

○ Tell your families how many guests they may invite. This prevents any problems and hurt feelings later.

○ Find out how much each side intends to contribute to the wedding, if anything, and what they intend their involvement to be.

It's also important for the bride and groom to practice their future marriage skill as a united front. It's easy to let family politics cause rifts between you as the stress of planning builds up, especially if the two families don't get along. Discuss any developing problems together, and try to solve them together. The patterns you set during your engagement will dictate how you interact with your families for the rest of your marriage.

Sad Story/Happy Ending

A bride was having a problem with her future mother-in-law adding people to the guest list with alarming frequency. The bride's list was well over what she started with, and the mother-in-law showed no indication of stopping. It even reached the point where the bride was going to have to cut her list to accommodate her mother-in-law's work associates, but she was afraid to say anything! Finally the groom stepped in and told his mother she was welcome to invite more guests if she didn't mind contributing to the wedding budget so they could accommodate her extra guests. Suddenly the mother's extra guests weren't as important as they had been, and the guest list shrank back to normal.

Setting the Style of the Wedding

After you have established an approximate date for the wedding, you need to give some thought to the style of celebration you want. It is important for you and your fiancé to take some time early on to determine what type of wedding suits you both. You can have a lovely wedding whether your style is caviar or Cheese Nips.

DON'T Forget the Marriage Because of the Wedding
Remember why you are getting married in the first place. Take breaks from wedding planning so you can refocus on the most important thing—each other. Once I had a couple who instituted "No Wedding Wednesdays" as the one day they couldn't talk about wedding plans. Now I suggest this to all my brides and grooms as a great sanity-saver!

Be Yourself

You need to take many factors into consideration when you're deciding on your personal wedding style, but always keep in mind that the wedding is a reflection of who you are as a couple. This is not the time to show off to your guests by using fingerbowls when you really eat off paper plates at home.

Defining Your Wedding Style

- ○ How do you like to entertain? Do you enjoy candlelight and fine wine or cookouts and microbrews?
- ○ Do you enjoy intimate gatherings for a few friends or festive cocktail parties for tons of people?
- ○ What type of weddings have you enjoyed most and why?
- ○ Would you define your personal taste as modern, casual, romantic, or formal?
- ○ What types of restaurants do you enjoy?

Your wedding is probably the biggest party you'll ever host, and good hosts make their guests feel comfortable. Take your fiancé, friends, and family into consideration as you envision your wedding day. Most important, be honest about the type of wedding that best suits you as a couple. Some of the loveliest weddings I've planned haven't been the most elaborate parties, but the ones that perfectly expressed the couple and made everyone feel comfortable and welcomed.

By the Numbers

Another big question that ties into the style of the wedding is how large an event you intend to throw. Be aware that the numbers you set early on influence many decisions farther on down the road. For instance, your guest list determines the type of reception site you can select. If you have a guest list of 200 people whom you must invite, an intimate seated dinner at a historic mansion is probably not in your future.

The number of people in the bridal party is another area many couples set without giving it the proper amount of thought. I've seen so many brides rush out and ask 10 of their dearest girlfriends to be in their wedding and then live to regret it as relationships change over the course of the planning.

DON'T **Succumb to the Reciprocated-Bridesmaid Pressure**

Just because you were in a friend's wedding does not mean you must ask her to be in yours. Friendships often change, and you might not be as close as you once were. Or you might be trying to keep your bridal party small. Whatever the reason, don't feel obligated. You can include someone in your wedding without putting her in dyed-to-match shoes.

Take your time to think about who really has been important in your life, and discuss it with your fiancé. The size of your bridal parties should be a mutual decision. You don't have to have equal numbers on both sides, but it will look odd if the groom has 3 attendants while the bride has 11.

Another crucial yet often-overlooked element of the bridal party is the financial one. Remember that if you have 10 bridesmaids, that means 10 bouquets and 10 attendant gifts, not to mention extras such as hotels, hair, and makeup you may choose to pay for. Bridal parties escalate a budget very quickly.

Take your time to ask friends to be in your wedding party. Before you make impulsive decisions, discuss with your fiancé the number of attendants you both envisioned and how your numbers impact your style of ceremony and budget. You can always add people, but once you have asked someone, it's difficult to un-ask them.

First Things First

Do	Don't
✓ Think carefully before you select a wedding date.	✗ Forget why you're getting married.
✓ Learn to compromise.	✗ Force a wedding style that isn't yours.
✓ Take your time when selecting your wedding party.	✗ Neglect to communicate clearly with your families.
✓ Determine the size of your wedding after careful thought.	✗ Invite everyone you know.

2

Look Before You Leap: Getting Organized

Now that you've made a few preliminary decisions about the overall style and scope of your wedding, it's time to get into the nitty-gritty of your wedding planning. This doesn't mean going out and buying the biggest wedding organizer you can lift without a special weight belt. This means setting a simple but detailed timeline of what needs to be done when. Before you begin booking sites and putting down deposits, it's important to have an overall vision of how the planning will unfold. In this chapter, I tell you how to prioritize tasks and how to get started the right way.

Drop That Wedding Checklist!

If you're anything like the typical bride, you've already been flipping through wedding magazines reading such terrifying articles as "One Thousand Things to Do Before Your Wedding" or "Two Million Great Favor Ideas to Make with Paper." Do yourself (and wedding planners everywhere) a favor: drop the magazines. Put down the 12-page to-do lists that instruct you on what to do every moment from now until your wedding day.

The problem with most of these lists is that they are too general because they have to fit everyone. I've said it before, and I'll say it again: wedding planning is not one-size-fits-all. If you use those generic lists, you must shrink or expand your own planning to fit into the mythical schedule allotted, and most of the time it just doesn't work the way it's proposed. I've seen too many brides go into a panic because they were behind schedule on some generic list that didn't even make sense for their wedding.

What's Important to You?

To make a customized wedding planning checklist for yourself that really works, you must first establish your planning priorities. Those priorities determine how you move forward with your planning. If you're dead set on having your ceremony at a very popular chapel that books up a year in advance, your wedding date will depend on the site's availability. If, however, you must get married on a specific date in June, you need to lock in that date and plan around it when finding sites and vendors. I've even had brides select a wedding date based on a favorite photographer's availability.

Setting Priorities

- ○ Decide the three or four elements of the wedding that are most important to you.

- ○ Determine what you will eliminate, such as favors or transportation for guests.

- ○ Decide the three or four elements that are least important to you, although you will include them.

- ○ What can you compromise on?

When you've come up with your personal wedding priorities, rank all the planning elements in order of importance to you. Have your fiancé make a list, as well. Ideally, you will merge these two lists into one master list of wedding priorities (no doubt after a certain amount of compromise and negotiation). This "most important" to "least important" list is the basis of your overall planning checklist. Of course, some things book up faster than others and might need to be moved to the front of the line if you want them at all.

Items to Book Early If You Want Them

○ **Specialty cars.** Those fancy Bentleys book up fast.

○ **Popular bands.** Again, the good ones go quickly.

○ **Top photographers.** Until human cloning comes along, the best photographers can only do one wedding per day.

○ **Popular reception sites.** Especially in the busy wedding months, the good places go first.

○ **Wedding gowns.** Unless you find one off the rack, allow 6 months to order one.

Timing Not to Ignore

Some elements of wedding planning have hard-and-fast dates, such as mailing of wedding invitations and getting licenses and permits. These things must be done at the right time regardless of how important they are to you.

DO Figure Out the Timing Early

It is important to set actual due dates for time-sensitive elements such as the wedding invitations. You don't want to be midway through the planning when you realize you didn't plan enough time to order the custom letterpress invitations you love and still mail them out in time.

It's usually best to work backward to determine when time-sensitive things must be taken care of. For example, wedding invitations should be mailed 6 to 8 weeks prior to the wedding, so count back from your wedding date to arrive at your mailing date. Then count back a week from there to find the date you need to have them back from the calligrapher so you can stamp and stuff them. Then count back from that date about 4 weeks to arrive at the date you need to give your envelopes to the calligrapher. To find the drop-dead date to actually order your invitations, just hop back about 3 weeks for thermography and 6 to 8 weeks for engraving or letterpress. That means you might need to order invitations 4 months before your wedding. Simple, right?

DON'T Forget the Tedious Stuff

Be sure to plan enough time to get your blood tests and marriage license, update passports, get visas for your honeymoon, and obtain any permits or insurance needed for your wedding. Find out what you need and how long it takes to process it and then put those dates in your checklist.

Break It Down

When you have your master priority list with all your drop-dead dates for invitations and licenses, you should break it up into digestible bits. Depending on how fast you need to plan your wedding, five to six major tasks per month is a reasonable goal. Naturally, you will need to do more the first month or two to lock in your most important elements. But after that, pace yourself.

Each larger task can also be broken down into smaller tasks so the whole list isn't so overwhelming. For instance, instead of writing down a huge task such as "Book caterer," write down "Research caterers,"

"Request proposals," and "Set up meetings." This also enables you to mark things off your list faster.

Aside from your month-by-month prioritized planning list, it is a great idea to add tasks to your day planner or Palm Pilot. This also helps you see if your wedding planning timeline meshes with your personal life. No sense kidding yourself that you'll have time to meet with photographers the same week you have to study for your medical board exams. Be realistic about your goals. The point of all this organization is to prevent you from having a breakdown, not put you on a fast track to one.

Share the Joy

Another great feature to add to your master to-do list is a column that assigns each task to a different person, most likely you or your fiancé. This helps divide the many wedding planning duties and gets your fiancé involved as well. Some things are natural to assign to him—selecting his formalwear and the gifts for the groomsmen, for example—but you might also want to ask him if he'd like to be involved with anything else in particular. Some grooms have a strong opinion on the band and take over that part entirely, while other grooms handle finding a cool getaway car.

DON'T Ask for an Opinion You Don't Want

Remember that if you ask for your fiancé's input, you need to take his wishes into consideration. I have seen so many brides harass their poor fiancés into attending floral appointments only to get upset when he voices an opinion different from hers. It is a smart bride who doesn't drag her groom along to every wedding appointment and lets him handle his planning duties without micro-managing him.

You can go even one step further and put a date by which each task needs to be completed. This is especially helpful as you get closer to the wedding day and more small tasks need to be knocked off the list. Be realistic when you set these dates, and don't crunch everything into the last 2 weeks and expect to emerge with your sanity intact.

Sad Story/Happy Ending

I am constantly harping on my clients to remember the 5-day waiting period we have in Washington, D.C., for marriage licenses. I once had a couple who almost didn't get married because they cut it so close. The groom put off getting his blood test for so long that they submitted their results exactly 5 days before the wedding. Of course it didn't occur to them that the license could be ready at any time on that fifth day, which happened to be their wedding day. Sure enough, the license wasn't ready until the end of the day, and the groom actually picked up the license on the way to his 6 o'clock wedding!

Your planning timeline should be customized to your priorities and the way you work. If you like to get lots done early, then by all means, plan merrily away. But also realize that just because an arbitrary list says you should select your florist at a certain time doesn't mean you're dead in the water if you don't. Design your planning to your own pace, and you'll be a much happier bride.

Let It Flow

Now that you've created a month-by-month timeline of your wedding planning, I need to give you a piece of wedding planner wisdom: don't worry if you don't do everything at exactly the right time. Aside from the drop-dead dates I discussed earlier in this chapter and your top priorities, your planning timeline should be a fluid document that adjusts to your needs and time. Don't let your timeline rule your life.

When you get started with the planning, some things naturally go faster than others, and some things might take a bit longer than you expected. This is okay. Usually you're waiting on contracts or proposals from vendors, and this might cause some tasks to drag into the next month. Don't have a nervous breakdown if you haven't checked an item off your list for April and it's already May. Now, if your calligrapher is waiting on your envelopes and they've been lost in the mail for a week already, you have my permission to have a minor meltdown.

Help Is on the Way

At this point in the game, you should make a decision whether or not you'll need to hire a professional wedding planner. It's best not to wait until you're knee-deep in wedding planning and realize you're lost to call a wedding planner.

Reasons to Hire a Wedding Planner—Pronto!

❍ You don't live in the area where you're getting married.

❍ You and your fiancé have demanding jobs and have no time to do the needed legwork.

❍ You live in a major city with so many options it would take you a year just to wade through them all.

❍ You don't have family or friends who can help you out.

❍ You are unorganized and have problems completing tasks.

Wedding planners have become more of a staple than a luxury over the past few years (especially in metropolitan areas), but not all weddings need a wedding planner. Be sure your budget can handle the cost; it doesn't make sense to spend a quarter of your overall budget on a wedding planner. Ideally, a wedding planner should come in at no more than 10 to 15 percent of your total budget. True, planners can save you money, but they aren't miracle workers. If most of your budget goes to their fee, they just won't have enough to work with.

Reasons You Might *Not* Need a Wedding Planner

○ You are a complete control freak who will micromanage everything your planner does and most likely drive her to drink. You know who you are.

○ You're looking for a scapegoat to blame things on if they go wrong. (I actually had someone tell me this is why they wanted to hire me. I passed on the wedding, as you can imagine.)

○ You have a mother or sister or girlfriend who is eager to take on a big role in the planning.

○ You live in a small town where there is one good florist, a handful of good reception sites, and your mother has used the same caterer for years.

○ You have lots of time to research and run around. The thought of hand-making your own favors warms your heart.

If you've determined you need a wedding planner, you have to find one who is the perfect fit for your budget and personality. Do your research, and be sure you've found the perfect fit before you sign a contract.

Calling All Wedding Planners ...

Probably the best way to find a planner is by word of mouth. Call the top hotels and wedding vendors in your area; who do they recommend? They see lots of wedding planners and know the great ones from the run-of-the-mill. Some professional organizations such as the Association of Bridal Consultants (ABC) and the International Special Events Society (ISES) have referral services where you can search for a qualified planner in your area. These organizations do have requirements for membership, so you're looking at a more qualified pool than you'd get by flipping through the phone book. You can also search online through the mega sites and other group wedding sites, but because these are paid placements, there's no way to determine who is great and who just hung out a shingle.

When you've narrowed down the list and gotten some names, it's time to do some research. Visit their websites, and read the information—it's there for a reason. When you feel like you know a little bit about the planner or the company, give them a call. Remember, in a lot of cases, the wedding planner is interviewing you just as much as you are interviewing them, so always be polite. Being impatient and snippy won't start things off on the right foot.

DO Educate Yourself

Wedding planners love when brides have taken the time to actually read the package information on our website and have questions prepared when they call. This shows the bride is proactive and will most likely approach all the wedding planning in a professional way.

It's nice to meet a consultant in person whenever possible. This is the best way to determine if your personalities will mesh well for the months of planning ahead of you. The first meeting with a planner is not a free planning session, though, so don't come to the meeting expecting to pump her for information or leave with a list of vendors to call. For you, the meeting is intended to be an introduction to the way she works, and for her, it is an information-gathering session about your wedding wishes and expectations.

What to Look for in a Wedding Planner

○ **Reputation.** Have you heard lots of good buzz about this company? Are they recommended by everyone you talk to? If you haven't heard anything about them, ask yourself why.

○ **Personality.** Be sure you get along with the planner you'll be working with. You need to like her from the beginning, because you'll be spending lots of time together.

○ **Ethics.** Be sure you understand how the process works and if the planner takes commissions from vendors. Different areas of the country have different operating procedures, but everyone you work with should be clear about her practices.

○ **Budget.** There are planners for all budgets, so find one who fits yours. If you can't hire a planner for your whole wedding, consider hiring one for part of the planning or a coordinator just for the wedding day.

Play Nice with Your Wedding Planner

Finding a wedding planner is a mutually selective process, so be respectful of her and her time. Don't call the day before and expect her to have a clear calendar, and don't expect weekends to be good for her, either. Remember that weddings happen on the weekends, so her workweek is just kicking into high gear on Friday!

Wedding planners work crazy hours because of their constant weekend work and the need to meet with clients after work (not to mention being in the office during regular office hours to get work done), so be on time to your appointment. Just because wedding planning is an extracurricular activity for you doesn't mean you shouldn't treat your wedding planner the way you would any other professional.

Look Before You Leap: Getting Organized

Questions to Ask a Wedding Planner

- ❍ How do you charge—flat fee, percentage of the total budget, or hourly?
- ❍ Are weddings your primary business or a sideline?
- ❍ How long have you been in business?
- ❍ What is included in the packages? What are any possible extra costs (overtime, assistants, etc.)?
- ❍ Do you take commissions from vendors?
- ❍ Who will I be working with? You exclusively or assistants? Who will be there on my wedding day?

After you've selected the perfect wedding planner, be sure to start out on the right foot. Never assume anything. If you want a weekly update on what she's doing for you, let her know up front. If you need help or advice with something outside her usual services, ask before you jump to the conclusion that she will handle it.

Read her contract carefully, and don't be afraid to add specifics if you feel it is too general. Having a line-itemed list of services to be provided by the consultant is a great way of clearing up any confusion. Don't fall into the trap of thinking that just because you've hired a planner for your wedding, she will help you with your rehearsal dinner, engagement party, bridal shower, bridesmaids' luncheon, and farewell brunch.

Ways to Work Well with a Wedding Planner

- ❍ Be clear about your expectations and any frustrations you may have.
- ❍ Be realistic. Sending your planner a long list of things you want her to do by the next day is unreasonable.

○ Don't call her 10 times a day with little questions. Save them for one call or, even better, e-mail her your list and you'll have your questions and her response in writing to refer to later.

○ Trust her to do things for you at the right time.

Although you may feel it's crucial to book your wedding day manicure 10 months out, your planner knows when it really needs to be taken care of. Trust her experience, and let her do her job.

Whether you hire someone to guide you through the planning or decide to brave it on your own, you need to be organized. Take time early on to make a realistic wedding checklist that reflects your personal priorities, and allow it to be flexible as you go along. Once you've done this, ignore all the other brides who try to convince you that if you haven't booked your hairdresser a year out, you're doomed. Those poor things are stuck with one of those generic magazine lists. Maybe you can give them a copy of this book as a prewedding present!

Getting Organized

Do	Don't
✓ Set wedding priorities and customize your planning.	✗ Follow a prefab planning checklist.
✓ Delegate planning tasks to your fiancé.	✗ Panic if you don't follow your timeline exactly.
✓ Hire a wedding planner if you need one.	✗ Be overly demanding or have unrealistic expectations of your wedding planner.

3

Is "Wedding Budget" an Oxymoron?

So now you know what to do and when to do it. The next big questions you ask should be "How much will it cost?" and "How are we going to pay for it?" Even though this chapter probably sounds about as much fun as a root canal, it is one of the most important. In these pages, I tell you what to expect in terms of wedding expenses, explain how to set a realistic budget, and give you tips on how to stay on budget. Most important, you learn how to avoid typical budgeting pitfalls and stay out of wedding debt.

It's Going to Cost *How Much?*

By far the biggest source of stress and shock in wedding planning is realizing how much this one day of celebration is going to set you back. This is particularly difficult for most grooms to comprehend. How could one day cost $10,000, $20,000, $40,000, and even more than $60,000? I'm sure it seems inconceivable at this point that you might spend that much on your wedding, but take it from me, it's easy to reach those numbers if you don't carefully think through your wedding budget.

Pooling the Funds

When figuring your wedding budget, the first thing you need to do is determine where the money is coming from and how much you can count on. Maybe your parents have offered to pay for the entire wedding (lucky girl!), or maybe they have given you a set amount to work with. I often see the groom's family contributing to the wedding as well, but this is not something you should expect unless it's offered. You and your fiancé should also determine how much, if anything, you'll contribute for your wedding and how you'll cover the costs.

DO **Know How You'll Cover Wedding Expenses**

Do you have enough savings to cover your contribution to the wedding, or will you need to start setting more back? It's a great idea to open a separate bank account to be used only for wedding expenses. This way you can begin putting your wedding savings in this account and you will know exactly what you spend for the wedding. Use credit cards and personal loans as a last resort. You don't want to start your married life in debt.

Keep in mind when you're accepting money for your wedding that you are also relinquishing a bit of the control. More often than not, I see families want a voice in the decision-making when they're paying. Money is power, and once you have accepted financial assistance for your wedding, you need to be prepared to accept family input and opinions as well. Of course there's a difference in the amount of control that can be exerted when your parents foot the entire bill than when they just give you a small contribution. I've had brides circumvent this problem by having their family pay for one specific element of the wedding. This lets the parents have input in that area but limits their control over the entire wedding.

Who Pays for What?

Traditionally, the majority of wedding expenses are covered by the bride's family with certain elements taken care of by the groom and his family. The rules have relaxed over the years, though, and couples are dividing up the expenses based on their own situations and their family's ability or willingness to contribute.

If there's any ambiguity concerning who will pay for what, it's better to get things out in the open as soon as possible. Have your fiancé broach the subject with his family if you don't feel comfortable bringing it up. Never ever demand anything. It is up to each side to determine what they can pay for, and it is your job to graciously accept.

Each area of the country also has its own set of rules regarding expenses. In some areas, it is customary for the groom to pay for the bridal bouquet, while in others it is common for the bride's family to pay for the bridesmaids' lodging. Take these customs into account when planning your budget.

What Goes In?

Unfortunately, there's no magic formula to create a personalized and realistic wedding budget. Like the planning timeline, budgets need to be customized according to your specific priorities, as well as other individual factors such as the area of the country you live in. Lots of magazines and websites provide charts of what you should spend in each area, but these are arbitrary figures and might have nothing to do with what really matters to you. By all means, make a sample budget on a wedding website for the sheer entertainment value, but don't expect it to be a realistic document unless you want to be pulling your hair out several months later.

Using a computer spreadsheet program such as Excel is a great way to keep track of expenses. Set it up early with estimated costs for all the items you want to include so you can see how realistic your budget really is. Include all the major wedding categories, as well as a line for tax and gratuity. Add a line for a 10 percent overage, or cushion, at the bottom. This should give you a rough idea of the realities of wedding expenses.

How comprehensive your wedding budget is is up to you, but you need to decide on what to include early on. Nothing is more maddening to a wedding planner than having brides add things once we're knee-deep in the planning and then expect the budget to be unaffected. If you intend to put the rehearsal dinner and honeymoon in your wedding budget, do it now. Be clear from the beginning on what your bottom line must include, and try not to tack things on as you go along. And if certain things aren't included in the wedding budget, be sure you know who will pay for them and how!

Usually Forgotten Items in a Wedding Budget

- Taxes and gratuities

- Gifts for attendants, parents, and each other

- Other parties, such as the rehearsal dinner or farewell brunch

- Staging, dance floors, portable restrooms, generators, and other nonglamorous rental equipment

- Hotel rooms for the bride and groom

- Licenses and permits

Make your budget as inclusive as possible from the beginning. If you think you might want to have favors or welcome bags for your out-of-town guests, put it in the budget. If you end up eliminating them, at least your budget will go down instead of creeping up like it will if you add them later on.

Factor It All In

One of the most common mistakes couples make when they decide how much they'll spend on their wedding is not factoring in all the elements. It is easy to decide you'll spend no more than $20,000, but it is quite another to hit that magic number when you haven't considered your guest count or other priorities. You can repeat your bottom line budget until you are blue in the face, but you won't be anywhere near it if you invite 50 additional guests or decide to upgrade the bar without thinking about how that impacts your wallet.

DON'T Budget Blindly

Before you begin putting down deposits, be sure you've broken down your budget so you can see exactly how much money is going to each element. You don't want to book an expensive photographer and band and then realize you haven't left any money for transportation or the wedding cake you've had your heart set on. Detail your budget so you know exactly how much you can spend *before* you start spending.

The first step to setting a budget is deciding how you will arrive at your bottom line. Will you start out with a firm number, or will you list your priorities and reach a number from there? If your parents are picking up the tab for the wedding, they might give you a figure to work with. If, however, you are paying for part of the wedding or your parents haven't given you a firm budget, you might need to do a little work to arrive at your total budget amount.

If you have a bottom line amount to work with, work backward to determine how much you have to spend in each area. Decide what is most important to you and what areas you want to focus your money on, and put those in your budget first. If it is crucial that you have a great band, allow more money for that. Be aware that you might have to cut back in another area to make it all work, though. Lose the idea that you must use every cute idea you've ever seen in a wedding magazine or your wedding won't be perfect.

DO **Be Prepared for Some Give and Take**

Unless you're one of those lucky few who have very large or unlimited budgets, you have to be willing to compromise to stay within your wedding budget. Knowing what elements of the wedding are important to you and what elements don't matter as much is so vital. I always tell my brides to pick a few areas of the wedding to focus their wedding money and creativity on instead of trying to spread themselves too thin by doing everything. People will remember what you do well.

Factors to Consider When You Set Your Budget

○ How many guests are on your guest list? Can this number be reduced?

○ What are the two or three most important elements of the wedding for you and your fiancé?

○ What is the bottom-line number, or what are you willing to spend?

○ What is not included in the budget, or what are you covering yourselves?

Don't forget that guest count is the single largest budget-buster and also the quickest way to cut back your budget. Determine early on if the extra guests are worth going over budget for or if you'd rather have a nicer wedding for fewer people. I often see brides who want it both ways. They want to serve the most expensive menu and don't want to cut back on their guest list, but they get very upset when they go over budget. You really can't have your cake and eat it, too.

Sticking to Your Budget

Now that you've set a realistic budget, I'm going to tell you how to do the impossible and stick to it. Most brides think that once they've set the budget the hard part is over. Guess what? The hard part is actually monitoring your spending as you go along so things never get out of hand.

Quick Tips for Staying on Budget

○ Review your budget at least once a month.

○ Add each new expense to your budget as soon as you place the deposit.

○ If you go over in one area, you must make up for it by coming in under budget in another.

○ Don't use up your cushion too quickly.

Out of Sight, Out of Control

You need to think of your budget as something fluid. Don't stick it in a drawer and forget about it for the rest of your engagement. Ideally, you should keep updating it each time you spend something on your wedding and each time you are considering a major expense. This way you'll know if you're on track every step of the way, and each financial decision you make will be a well-informed one.

It All Adds Up

You also need to limit the number of little things you add on. It's so easy to forget that the little expenses add up quickly, and they can end up putting you way over budget. I once had a bride who insisted that additions that cost less than a thousand dollars were easy add-ons and she didn't want to worry about them despite my warnings that this wasn't a good idea! Guess who had a panic attack when her budget went sky high?

Sad Story/Happy Ending

As a wedding planner, one of the more common problems I encounter is a bride calling me for help once she has already started planning her wedding and gotten in over her head. One bride called me in a panic because she'd already booked an expensive reception site, one of the area's top photographers, and a pricey band without doing an overall budget for her wedding. After realizing that she'd spent a big chunk of her entire wedding budget on just three things, she nearly had a nervous breakdown and hired me to get her back on track. Luckily, she was willing to be flexible and creative with the rest of her planning, and we were able to put together a fabulous cocktail party reception with tons of dancing and still stay within the amount her parents had given her. It is much easier to start out the right way, though!

Beware of the tendency to see your budget as just numbers on a page. This is money you will have to come up with at some point. It isn't *Monopoly* money, so don't start signing contracts and charging expenses on your credit card without looking at the big picture. An even better idea is to be sure you have the money in your wedding account before you spend it. Be sure you're earning points or miles when you use credit cards, and try to pay them off each month (or at least don't max them out before you're halfway through the planning). Allocating one credit card for wedding expenses is another easy way to keep track of what you spend. Check on the consumer protection policy on the card you choose. This can be a big asset if you have issues with a wedding vendor down the road.

Is "Wedding Budget" an Oxymoron?

DO — Include the Necessities and the Extras

Be sure you've included taxes and gratuities in your budget. Consider wedding insurance if you're worried about something going terribly wrong. These policies cover your expenses if you must postpone your wedding due to illness or if a hurricane destroys your reception site. If you decide you just can't go through with the wedding, though, the insurance company won't help you.

Budgeting

Do	Don't
✓ Talk with your families about your budget.	✗ Start spending before you set a budget.
✓ Prioritize and compromise.	✗ Forget to update your budget.
✓ Make a comprehensive budget from the start.	✗ Neglect to add taxes and gratuity.

4

How Not to Wipe Out on the Wedding Web

The Internet is probably the single biggest factor in revolutionizing the wedding industry (after Martha Stewart, of course). Brides can practically plan their entire wedding without leaving the comfort of their home, or at least do a ton of research before setting out. However, you do need to be a bit careful when surfing the wedding web. In this chapter, I fill you in on the best ways to get information and shop online. Plus, I give you the nitty-gritty on wedding chat sites and how they might hurt you more than help you.

Surfing and Sifting Through Wedding Websites

One of the best ways to understand the wedding industry and see what is out there and available is to hop online. The wedding planning industry has become almost completely reliable on virtual information. Brochures and mailings are practically a thing of the past, because you can get more current information via websites.

With that said, you do need to be aware when you're researching or shopping online. A great website doesn't necessarily mean a great product or service, so be careful and protect yourself.

Web Guidelines

○ Beware of sites you must pay to join. The best sites are free!

○ Use credit cards in case you need to return products or take consumer action against an online vendor.

○ Be sure all e-commerce transactions are secure. Never e-mail your credit card information through an unsecured site.

You can do research online in several ways. Mega-sites such as The Knot (www.theknot.com) and the Wedding Channel (www.weddingchannel.com) have become enormous industries within themselves, even putting out guidebooks and magazines. Smaller group sites don't have the vast resources of the mega-sites. These are usually tailored to listing vendors and are often more regional. Then you have a slew of independent sites for everything from wedding planners to favors. How do you know where to go?

The Mega-Sites

The first stop on your virtual shopping tour should be to one of the mega-sites. Check out The Knot, the Wedding Channel, Brides (www.brides.com), or Modern Bride (www.modernbride.com)—just for the experience, if nothing else!

Mega-Site Browsing Tips

○ Take some of the budgeting advice with a grain of salt. It has to be pretty general to cover the whole country, so it may not be completely realistic for your area. Some of it has made me giggle myself silly. (See Chapter 3 for more on realistic wedding budgets.)

○ Don't obsess over the timelines. Each planning process is unique, and a site that caters to thousands of brides can't be tailored to your specific needs.

How Not to Wipe Out on the Wedding Web

○ Just because a vendor is linked to the sites doesn't mean it's good (although many of them are wonderful, and I use them myself). Always remember that these links are paid for.

○ Beware of the slew of marketing information you may get from the site's partners.

The Knot (www.theknot.com) has become famous as one of the first major wedding sites and now has extensive vendor resources, budgeting and planning worksheets, and oodles of stuff to buy online. You can find just about anything on this site, including the infamous Knotties (Knot chat board aficionados).

The Wedding Channel (www.weddingchannel.com) is another megasite with resources galore. The most unique feature of this site is the comprehensive registry. If you register at any one of more than a dozen stores, your registry is automatically linked to the Wedding Channel. This is an enormous convenience for friends and family located all over the country. I never go into a brick-and-mortar store to buy wedding gifts anymore.

Aside from the state-of-the-art registry, the Wedding Channel also features vendor links customized to your area, as well as a create-your-own-wedding-website feature. You won't find the extensive chat boards, but that isn't always a bad thing. (More on both of those later in this chapter.)

DO Take Advantage of the Internet's Convenience
You can update and check your registries from the Wedding Channel without ever setting foot in a store. This is a great way to keep tabs on things and will save you lots of time!

The Others

Aside from the monster sites, you can find numerous group sites on the web. These may be tailored to your specific region and highlight tons of local vendors, such as The Washington DC Wedding Guide (www.dcwed.com) and The Maryland Wedding Guide (www.marylandweddings.com) do in my area. Or they may be general sites geared toward different types of weddings such as www.TwoBrides.com and www.TwoGrooms.com, which are designed to help people planning commitment ceremonies throughout the country. These sites can be great because they may be more specialized and less general. Sites that focus on one region or city usually have a broad selection of vendors to choose from instead of just a smattering.

Some of the smaller group sites are also more selective and exclusive. The website for *Grace Ormonde Wedding Style* magazine (www.weddingstylemagazine.com) is a perfect example of a very high-end magazine that has launched a website with only very select wedding vendors profiled. This site is also a fabulous source of truly cutting-edge wedding style.

DON'T Rely on the Web Exclusively

A website is a great way to get an idea of services offered and quality of work. It isn't a foolproof way to shop, though. Use the web to prescreen vendors, but don't make final decisions without meeting or talking to the vendor. I know some wedding vendors who have stellar websites but aren't the greatest to work with. Nothing beats an in-person meeting!

Vendor Sites

Almost every wedding vendor today has a website as a way to promote themselves. If I meet someone who doesn't have one, it makes me wonder (this doesn't necessarily apply if you live in a smaller town that is more referral based than web based)! Lots of these individual sites are linked to one or more group sites, whether it is one of the big boys or a smaller, exclusive site.

To Chat or Not to Chat?

Another huge component of today's wedding websites is the message boards. The Knot is known for its "Knotties," brides who spend lots of time on the message boards debating everything from which vendor to hire to where to buy the perfect unity candle. These boards can be packed with information, but they can also be overwhelming.

Read with a Grain of Salt

The first thing you should remember if you choose to delve into the world of wedding chat is that these people are not experts. They are brides just like you. Sure, they may be very opinionated brides who seem to know everything, but they are not professionals. Sometimes it can be very helpful to get the opinion of another bride, but always remember that it's her opinion. She does not have years of wedding-planning experience to back up her opinion.

Beware: Chatting Can Be Dangerous

Be forewarned that vendors are very aware of what brides are saying, and they don't always take it lightly. Don't use the boards as a soapbox against a vendor you didn't like. If the vendor was unethical or performed very poorly, however, it is fair to post a simple warning if you are prepared to back it up with evidence. Save the ranting diatribes for when you are behind closed doors!

What *Not* to Say on a Message Board

○ Never say anything you wouldn't want the world to know. These are not private forums, and it is easier than you'd think to figure out your identity.

○ Never trash a vendor without lots of just cause and evidence. Actually, it is smart never to trash a vendor for any reason, because it is a small industry and word gets around. Being accused of slander is not a pretty thing, and no one will want to work with you.

○ Don't use these boards to complain about your fiancé, future mother-in-law, or bridesmaids. It is just in bad taste and can easily come back to bite you in the butt. I've seen it happen, girls.

○ Don't get involved in the catfights that can break out online. There can be a mob mentality to being able to attack people anonymously.

DON'T Think People Aren't Listening

One of the best examples of the danger of wedding chat boards I've heard came from an exclusive wedding photographer friend. He'd had a good meeting with a bride and was expecting to shoot her wedding. Before he signed the contract, he heard from another wedding vendor (who reads the chat boards) that a bride was posting lots of requests for "picks and pans" about him. He was so upset that this bride was soliciting negative comments and dirt about him that he refused to shoot her wedding.

The Pros and Cons of Virtual Shopping

I must admit that I have found some of the cutest wedding accessories imaginable by surfing online. If you know what you're doing, you can save yourself hours of driving from store to store hunting down an elusive item. Being a smart online shopper can be one of the keys to keeping your wedding sanity.

Online Shopping Rules

○ Give yourself plenty of time. Order early so if something doesn't fit or look like you expected you still have time to find something else.

○ Print out all your online receipts and keep them.

○ Call and ask for samples if you're unsure of a color. Some sites will send samples of paper products or fabrics. Not all will do this, but it's worth asking about.

○ Factor in the shipping time. If you're in a rush, be sure to get expedited shipping and an estimated arrival date. Remember to get a tracking number so you can monitor your package en route.

Sad Story/Happy Ending

One of my favorite brides was having a wedding in October with a fall leaf theme. Every detail featured beautiful fall leaves, including the hand-painted aisle runner. Unfortunately, when the aisle runner arrived 2 weeks before the wedding, it was not at all what the bride had envisioned and the artist refused to do a new one. I quickly went online and did a search for custom aisle runners and found The Original Runner Co. (www.OriginalRunner.com) in New York City. They had great references and had done some pretty high-profile weddings, so I called them as soon as they opened. Luckily, they were nice as could be and agreed to do a rush order aisle runner for us. It turned out to be even more stunning than the bride had hoped!

There are online shopping sites for just about everything you can imagine, from shoes to invitations to favors. You can find great sources on the group wedding sites and links from other individual sites, too. If you have a specific item in mind, such as silver place card holders, type those key words in a search engine, and you'll get lots of great sources. Check out the resource appendix in the back of this book for my favorite online wedding stores.

eBay (www.ebay.com) is also a resource for great wedding bargains, if you're a savvy bidder. There you can find an amazing number of wedding gowns available, as well as just about any other bridal accessory you can imagine. Just be sure you know the site's policies and rules of engagement before you get sucked into this addictive world of competitive shopping.

www.[Your Names Here].com

One of the fastest-growing trends in weddings today is personal wedding websites. Brides and grooms can create personal websites to give their guests every bit of information about the wedding in one place. Personal sites started as a feature of some of the mega-sites, but now it is common for couples to get a domain name and design their own (or even hire a designer).

I have to say I'm a big fan of these sites. For one, you can pack much more information on a website than you can in a mailing. Your invitation shouldn't be cluttered with tons of travel information and maps, although it is still a good idea to include the basic information on hotels in your invitation or save-the-date card for those who aren't web savvy. Use the website for more comprehensive information that just won't fit on a 3×5 wedding enclosure.

How Not to Wipe Out on the Wedding Web

Information to Always Include on Your Website

○ The pertinent details such as dates, times, and locations for each event. A schedule for the wedding weekend is always helpful, although if some events aren't open to all guests (such as the rehearsal dinner) don't include that for everyone to see. It will only cause confusion.

○ The contact information for area hotels you've selected to host your out-of-towners.

○ Your contact information in case guests have any questions or problems.

○ Transportation details or maps and directions.

Do you have to have a website? Of course not. But think of it as a way to save yourself plenty of time and headaches answering the same questions from a hundred guests. I have brides who send out adorable save-the-date postcards to their guests with just their wedding date and wedding website. They put everything else on their site and let guests surf at will.

DO Let Your Website Reflect Your Personalities

Have fun with your website! Include a musical clip from your band, some fun engagement pictures of the two of you, or the story of how you met. One couple included light-hearted bios of their wedding party on their website. Even if your wedding is formal, your website can be fun.

If you don't want to spend money on building a site (or would have as easy a time designing a rocket ship as a website), you can still get your wedding online. Mega-sites such as The Knot and the Wedding

Channel offer free websites you can personalize to a certain degree. The best part is that they take about 5 minutes to set up, and you can easily add content as you go along.

The Wedding Web

Do	Don't
✓ Use the Internet to prescreen vendors.	✗ Hire anyone based on their website alone.
✓ Chat with caution.	✗ Take chat room advice as expert opinion.
✓ Take advantage of online shopping convenience.	✗ Wait until the last minute to make Internet purchases.
✓ Use personal websites to give your guests more wedding details.	✗ Feel you must spend a bundle on a custom website.

5

The Search Is On

Now that you've laid the groundwork for your wedding planning, it's time to get out there and find the perfect place for your once-in-a-lifetime event. In this chapter, I clue you in on how to find the perfect venue that will elevate your wedding from ordinary to truly fabulous, as well as give you the pros and cons of different types of sites. Whether you lock down the ceremony site or the reception first depends on your wedding planning priorities. Either way, you need to work on finding both sites in tandem so you won't find yourself with the perfect chapel reserved and no place to hold the reception.

Going to the Chapel: The Search for the Perfect Ceremony Site

You might be one of those lucky brides who has always known she will get married in her hometown church, and securing your ceremony site is as easy as making one call to the church secretary. If so, kick back, relax, and breeze right over this section.

But if you're like most of my brides, you haven't grown up in the city where you'll be married and you have no clue what your options are. And today there are many places to hold a beautiful ceremony aside from the traditional religious venues.

The Traditional Choices

If getting married in a church, synagogue, or mosque is important to you, you have successfully narrowed down your options. The easiest scenario is that you attend the place where you'd like to get married. In the best of all possible worlds, you know the priests and love the sanctuary. Unfortunately, this isn't always the case.

If you don't attend a church or even know any you like but still envision getting married in one, you have the not-so-enviable task of church shopping. You can look in the phone book or even drive around to find places that fit your religious requirements. Not all places of worship are keen on brides calling around for churches like they would for caterers, so use a great deal of tact. It's best if you can visit a church at least once so you will have some specific knowledge when you call.

Be warned that some churches are very warm and welcoming to non-members and others might be offended by your call. Be as polite as possible, and always thank whomever you speak with for his or her time. This is not a place of business, so throw out the concept that the consumer is always right. Churches are first and foremost a place of worship, not a wedding factory.

Questions to Ask at a Religious Site

○ Do you have to be a member to get married?

○ Are there any time constraints? Many Catholic churches require 6 months' lead time for weddings.

○ Do they require any premarriage counseling or courses?

○ Must you use their celebrants, or do they allow co-officiating? Must you use their musicians?

○ What are the fees and rules?

Once you've located a church that will agree to marry you and has your wedding date and time available, you need to get a copy of their rules and regulations. Find out what your responsibilities are and what restrictions your site has on things such as décor, music, and photography. Give copies of the ceremony site rules to all your vendors involved in the ceremony. Your florist will prefer to know that she can't attach anything to the pews before she arrives with a dozen pew decorations she can't use.

DO **Follow the Rules**

If your church requires that only religious music be played for the ceremony, don't try to sneak your favorite Beatles tune past them. Always respect the rules of the house of worship you have chosen.

If your ceremony site assigns you a wedding coordinator, be sure to defer to her expertise. Now listen up, ladies. This goes even if you've hired your own wedding coordinator! An independent wedding coordinator should be able to work with the church coordinator without stepping on her toes. I always love when a church has its own coordinators because she knows absolutely everything about the church and the minister—more than I could learn in the few hours I'm there, for sure! Listen to what she has to say, and play nice.

Off the Beaten Path: Other Ceremony Site Options

If you don't see yourself getting married in a religious setting, you still have lots of options. It's very common for my brides to have their ceremony and reception in the same place. You can't beat the convenience, and you don't have to worry about moving folks hither and yon.

If you want to have your wedding in a hotel, you can have the ceremony in a smaller ballroom or sometimes an outside courtyard and then move into a bigger space for the reception. Or you can have the ceremony and reception in the same room, and it can be "turned" (the industry term for resetting the room for the next event) during the cocktail hour. If you've chosen a historic mansion with gardens, you can opt for a ceremony in the garden and the reception inside the house. Or even hold the entire event outside.

Considerations for an Outdoor Ceremony

○ Is there any traffic noise from nearby highways or even airplanes?

○ Will there be enough light at the time you've chosen for your wedding, or will you need to bring in additional lighting?

○ Will you need to bring in a portable microphone so your guests can hear your vows?

○ Will you need to provide shade from direct sunlight for your guests and musicians? (Some won't play uncovered.)

○ What is your rain plan?

Occasionally, I have couples who get married in a separate garden setting and then move to a hotel or museum for the reception. This can be a lovely way to combine two very different styles, but it will require more logistics regarding transportation and setup. And you'll be paying two site fees.

Reception Sites: The Best Fit

Finding a site that fits your guest count, reception style, and personal taste isn't as easy as it may seem. Before you fall in love with the cozy historic home that can in no way fit your 200 guests, take some time to establish some of your venue criteria. By knowing your event's particular needs, you will be able to narrow down the field much faster and save lots of time you can better spend obsessing over the perfect wedding shoes.

Creating Your Venue Profile

○ How many guests will be attending?

○ Will your reception be fully seated, offer partial seating, or be primarily a stand-up cocktail party?

◯ Will the food be plated, served at several stations, placed on a buffet, or passed by waiters?

◯ If you are seating all of your guests, is it important that everyone be in one room with the music and dancing?

◯ Are you willing to tent an outdoor space, or do you despise tented receptions?

From your answers to these questions, you can determine exactly the type of spaces that will work for your reception. For instance, if you insist on having all 200 guests seated in the same room for dinner, very few historic homes will accommodate you. Your group would be better off in a hotel ballroom or in a spacious museum. If you have your heart set on a historic mansion, you might be able to seat your guests in a large tent attached to the house.

The style of reception plays a big role as well. A cocktail reception can easily fit in most spaces and is perfect for cozy historic homes, but a stand-up reception for 100 guests might get lost in a very large museum or ballroom. As you research sites, find out how many people they can hold for seated receptions and also standing ones. Don't try to fit your reception into a venue that doesn't work. It will result in an awkward flow to the entire party.

Avoiding the Cookie-Cutter Reception Site

One of the most frequent requests I get (aside from how to deal with future mother-in-laws) is to find a location for a bride that will make her wedding different from every other wedding she's ever attended. *Gulp*. No one wants their wedding to be just like everyone else's, and often the site is the biggest factor brides use to set their weddings apart.

Depending on where you live, you have lots of options for wedding receptions. Some towns have only a few ballrooms and spaces for rent, while larger cities might have hundreds of options ranging from modern lofts to botanical gardens.

Ways to Find Great Reception Venues

○ **Word of mouth.** Where do the top caterers and photographers love to work?

○ **The web.** Try the mega-sites as well as local ones.

○ **Magazines.** *Grace Ormonde Wedding Style* magazine includes top sites for major areas in its Five Star Directory. Other magazines such as *I Do* or *Modern Bride,* which have editions tailored to regions, are good sources, as well as industry publications such as *Locations* and *Agenda*.

○ **Bridal shows.** Although they can be madhouses, you can find some good sources at bridal shows if you can survive the crowds and weed through the glut of information.

If you're looking for one-stop shopping, run right for the hotels, reception halls, and clubs. Talk about making your job (and mine!) easy. These sites provide the space and (almost always) the catering, staff, and equipment. Some clubs and halls even have packages that include décor and music. Because this is all packaged together, you are often getting a better deal. The trade-off for all this convenience is that sometimes the receptions look and feel prepackaged.

The Advantages of Hotels

Hotels are my favorite of the all-in-one reception options because they are so service-oriented, especially in the luxury properties. There's nothing prepackaged about a wedding reception at the Ritz-Carlton, that's for sure. The top hotels offer upgraded linen and china, as well as world-class food and amazing service, so you never feel like you are in a wedding factory. Not all hotels have these upgrades to offer, so if you want your reception to look special in a Budget Inn, you might have to rent your own linens and china and do a little extra work to get the look.

Amenities Hotels Usually Offer

○ Space for the reception, and even the ceremony if you'd like.

○ In-house catering and a well-trained staff. Plus all the booze and bartenders.

○ All the equipment you'll need, including linens, tableware, and votive candles.

○ Discounted rooms for your guests and a suite for you.

○ The wedding cake (not at all hotels).

Another advantage to hotels—and it can be a big one—is that all your guests can stay in the same place as the reception. If you're holding a wedding in the hotel, you will get a special rate on your guest's rooms and, most likely, a complimentary suite for you and your fiancé on the wedding night. If you're lucky, you might also get complimentary rooms for your parents. This can be a big convenience and savings.

Because hotels are large spaces and often have multiple ballrooms, it's possible to have more than one wedding booked each day. If it will upset you to share your space with another bride, ask up front how many weddings the hotel holds and how they plan to keep the weddings from crossing paths.

Off to the Club

Private clubs also offer lots of packaged services, usually without the option of sleeping rooms for your guests. For members of private clubs (and sometimes the guests of members), the savings can be significant over hotel prices. Some clubs are stricter than others concerning nonmember use, so always check the club rules to see if holding your reception there is even an option.

Questions to Ask at a Private Club

○ What are the fees and requirements if you aren't a member?

○ Will the event space be private, or will club members be walking through?

○ What are the options for linens, chairs, and china?

○ Are there noise restrictions or cutoff times for music and the overall reception?

○ Are there cake cutting fees, parking fees, or corkage fees?

Some beautiful country clubs offer food and service comparable to top hotels, but not all of them do, so ask around and be sure the club you're considering has a good reputation. Visit the club and be sure it is maintained well. Clubs get lots of daily use by members, so they can get worn down quicker than hotels that have only a few events each week.

DON'T Assume a Private Club Is Off-Limits

Just because a club is private, doesn't mean you can't host an event there. Many clubs require a member to sponsor you, but often they help you find a willing member. Private clubs need revenue, too. Don't be afraid to ask how restrictive their rules are before you dismiss the option entirely.

What's in a Hall?

If you say the phrase *wedding hall* in Washington, D.C., you'll get a blank look in return. No such animal exists for us. In other parts of the country, however, wedding halls are a common and convenient option. At their best, they are venues geared almost entirely toward weddings and have the process down to a science. They can provide everything from the food to the flowers to the cake to the music. The downside can be that the weddings can feel mass produced.

Ways to Dress Up a Wedding Hall

○ Bring in your own linens, china, crystal, and even chairs from an event rental company.

○ Bring in your own florist, or upgrade from the package centerpiece offered. Don't even let the thought of balloons cross your mind.

○ Ask if menus can be customized. Come up with some creative and personalized food and specialty drinks.

○ Opt out of any standard offerings you don't like, such as risers for the wedding party, king and queen chairs for the bride and groom, or (God forbid!) fountains under the wedding cake. Don't be forced into anything you don't like.

Other halls available in some communities are just that: empty halls for rent. You bring in everything, from the caterer to the tables and chairs. This gives you more control but is as much work as an off-site wedding. You lose the convenience of the one-stop shopping that makes most hotels, clubs, and halls so appealing.

A Cultural Experience

Museums can be a wonderful and unique place to hold a wedding. Many metropolitan areas have huge museums that can hold large weddings and are a great alternative to ballrooms. Smaller museums can also be warm and intimate places for a reception—and a great way to introduce your guests to some area history or art.

Because the museum's primary concern is their exhibits, be very clear on all the rules and restrictions before you sign on the dotted line. Don't book a museum and then get upset later when you realize you can't serve your favorite red wine at dinner. Be prepared to play along with their rules.

Potential Museum Restrictions to Ask About

○ Do they allow you to take food and drink into galleries? Are red wine or red berries allowed?

○ Are there rules prohibiting candles or other décor (like fabric draping)?

○ Are there noise restrictions or time limits for music?

○ Are docents and security provided, and what is the cost?

A Little Piece of History

Historic homes and mansions are natural venues for weddings because they can be so charming and romantic. They can also be run down and impractical, so choose wisely. Don't fall head over heels for a gorgeous mansion and overlook potential wedding nightmares.

Potential Problems with Historic Homes

○ They may not be handicap-accessible. If you have guests in wheelchairs who won't be able to get up steps or into bathrooms, this is a big problem.

○ They may not have top-notch air conditioning or heat or even enough power circuits for your band. These are really old homes, after all.

○ They may have limited kitchen facilities or space. This will affect your caterer more than you, but it might change the type of service they can do well. Doing a plated dinner in a galley kitchen leads to grumpy chefs.

○ They might have rules regarding red wine and red foods, as well. Say good-bye to cosmopolitans (and hello to white cosmos)!

Usually, stand-up receptions or buffets with casual seating through-out the house work best in historic mansions. Because most houses are broken up into several smaller rooms, it's more practical to spread the food and drink in different areas and have people mingle. Trying to do a seated dinner when guests are scattered in 10 different rooms makes for a choppy reception.

Remember also to match your reception style to your site. There are few things worse than a wedding that has been shoehorned into the wrong venue.

There's No Place Like Home

At-home weddings can be charming and intimate—and a complete headache! Although you might think nothing could be simpler than hosting your reception at your home, nothing could be further from the truth. I've had clients who had to re-landscape their entire backyards to be able to fit a tent large enough for a wedding reception, not to mention the redecorating or cleaning people feel compelled to do before they invite a hundred or so guests into their home. At-home weddings always end up being more complicated than when they started out!

Considerations for At-Home Weddings

○ **Cost of bringing it all in.** You will most likely have to rent everything, from china and crystal to tents to generators.

○ **Parking.** Where will all these cars go? You will definitely need valet for large events and maybe even a permit. At the very least, you should kiss up to your neighbors before blocking their street with dozens of cars.

○ **Bathrooms.** Unless you're Aaron Spelling, you probably don't have enough bathrooms for a large wedding. You will need to bring in restroom trailers to supplement (not those Port-a-Johns, please).

○ **Setup and cleanup.** Think of the cost of bringing in a gardener and maid to get your house and lawn in shape before the wedding and then the repair and clean team that will need to come back when it's all over. Or, heaven forbid, the exhaustion of doing it yourself.

If you are thinking of having 20 close friends in your living room for champagne and cake, that's a different matter entirely. Your house could be the perfect spot for a very intimate reception, but it still requires a little more legwork or expense on your part.

The Great Outdoors

Nothing holds quite the same appeal as a garden wedding—when the weather is nice, of course. There is no greater disaster than a bride who had her heart set on a garden wedding and gets a hailstorm. I get an ulcer each time I do an outdoor wedding because so much depends on things out of my control.

Must-Haves for an Outdoor Wedding

○ **A rain plan.** If you don't have a covered option in case of bad weather, it is almost guaranteed to pour buckets. Also be aware of strong sun and heat. Don't make your guests swelter under a boiling summer sun without any shade.

○ **An appointed time and person to make the weather call.** Talk with all your vendors prior to the wedding, and find out the latest time you can make the call to move the event inside. Then designate who will make the decision (whether it will be you, your wedding planner, or your caterer), and inform everyone who will be making the call.

○ **The right equipment.** Be sure your tent has sidewalls you can put up in case of blowing rain, and pack some umbrellas in the car.

○ **The right gear.** Aside from rain, the outdoors can bring bugs and blistering sun. Stock up on bug spray (for the grass where people will be standing and the legs of the dining tables so bugs don't crawl up in search of food), fabric softener sheets to put under chair cushions to ward off mosquitoes, sunscreen under your makeup if you'll be standing outside a lot, and paper fans for guests if it will be warm.

The most important thing to have when you're planning a garden reception is flexibility and a sense of humor. You just can't control the weather, and the more you obsess about having a perfect summer day, the more miserable you'll be when it doesn't turn out quite as planned. Be prepared, and roll with the punches (or thunderclouds).

Sad Story/Happy Ending

As one of my brides was getting ready for her ceremony outside in a hotel courtyard, I noticed black clouds in the distance. As they got closer and darker, I made the call to pull the ceremony inside. Good thing, too! The skies opened up and it poured all night long. The courtyard where we were planning to hold the ceremony was flooded to the point that the bistro tables and chairs were bobbing around. Water even started to come in the hotel under the doors and through the overhead light fixtures (don't ask me how!). The florist quickly re-created the garden theme in the hotel's ballroom, and the ceremony went ahead on time with the sound of dripping water masked by the string quartet. The bride was easygoing enough to laugh it off and have a wonderful time despite the spring flood!

All Aboard!

Ships and boats obviously aren't options in all areas, but they can be creative venues for weddings. If you love the water, exchanging vows on the deck of a beautiful paddlewheel boat might be your idea of heaven. Keep in mind that not all your guests will be as seaworthy as you, though, and once the boat has set sail, there's no getting on or off. If you decide on a shipboard wedding, try to make it shorter than a typical 5-hour reception to be considerate of guests who might not want to be on the water that long. Seasickness patches aren't a bad thing to stock up on, either!

DO Be Specific

Let your guests know on the invitation or enclosures what time the boat will depart and from what dock. Unlike at most weddings, your guests won't be able to show up late!

Depending on your area, you might have other creative options. Maybe you live in a city with some great lofts or you live in wine country with a dozen vineyards at your disposal. I've seen weddings in castles, farms, orchards, and historic ruins. Be creative when looking for sites, and don't be afraid to hold your wedding somewhere just because it hasn't been done before. Just be sure to ask lots of questions and prepare for every possibility.

Ceremony and Reception Sites

Do	Don't
✓ Be respectful of church rules.	✗ Let churches know you're shopping around.
✓ Consider all-in-one venues if convenience and ease are important.	✗ Be afraid to look for unusual and unique sites.
✓ Have a bad-weather plan.	✗ Let bad weather spoil your wedding day.

6

Catering: It's Not Just Chicken Anymore

After you have your reception site locked in, you can start shopping around for caterers (or start working with your in-house caterer). It's important to know how to approach caterers and what to ask them. In this chapter, I clue you in on how to decipher catering lingo and the mystery of pricing. Most important, you learn what to focus your catering dollars on and what things not to bother with.

Selecting an Off-Site Caterer

If you're lucky, your reception site will have a list of approved or recommended caterers for you to select from. This makes it a lot easier to narrow down the field (and you're sure to get a caterer who knows your site well). If your site doesn't have a list, ask who they think does the best job on weddings at their venue. If you still need more names, you can turn to magazines and the Internet. But referrals are always better.

Narrow your search to three to five caterers maximum. Any more will be confusing and overwhelming. You want to have all your ducks in a row before you start calling around. Nothing drives a caterer crazy more than a bride calling without a reception site, with a vague guest count, and with no clue what type of reception she wants to have. Some caterers have generic menus for buffets, stations, and plated dinners for you to look at, but most (and most of the best ones) prefer to do a customized menu proposal.

What a Caterer Will Want to Know

○ Your guest count. This will affect the pricing a lot.

○ Your reception site. They need to know the space they will
   have and any logistical issues that might affect their staffing.

○ Your budget for catering.

○ What type of meal you wish to serve: buffet, stations, plated
   dinner, or passed hors d'oeuvres only. Mention favorite foods,
   allergies, and any foods you don't want to serve.

The Catering Proposal

If you present caterers with organized information that shows you
have given it some thought, you'll get better service and proposals
that will fit your needs better. Don't expect caterers to be able to get
customized proposals to you the next day, though. It usually takes a
week or more (depending on the time of year and their workload) to
put together creative menus with pricing that reflects your needs.

What to Expect in a Catering Proposal

○ An itemized list. Be sure you know how much you are paying
   for service, rentals, tax, food, and liquor.

○ The correct date, time, and duration of the reception; number of guests; and location. If any of these change throughout
   the planning process, let your caterer know!

○ Descriptions of the food to be served. If you're serving a
   dessert buffet, the proposal should specify the types of
   desserts offered.

○ Cancellation policy and the payment schedule.

Back to the Drawing Board

When you've gotten several proposals, how do you know who to choose? Usually, I find that one or two proposals come closer to what the bride had in mind and one or two are completely off the mark. Maybe the food sounds more appetizing on one or the pricing is much better on another. Try to narrow your choices down to two (no more than three) proposals that you really like to revise and rework.

DON'T Share Information

Don't be guilty of showing one caterer's proposal to another caterer. Even if you love a menu item one caterer proposed, it is unethical to take it to someone else to reproduce. If caterers find out what you're up to, you'll instantly be elevated to uber-Bridezilla status.

When you start the process of revising proposals with caterers, give them as much feedback as possible. Tell them what items you loved and which ones didn't blow your skirt up. Suggest new items you may have come up with as well. If pricing is an issue, mention this and ask for ways to trim the budget. It helps if you tell your caterer what areas you'd be willing to sacrifice to bring the budget down, as well.

Meeting Caterers

It's also a good idea to meet the catering executive once you've narrowed down to a couple options but before signing a contract. Don't expect your preliminary meeting with a caterer to be a tasting, though. Save that for when you are further along in the process. Use this initial meeting to get to know the caterer's personality and gauge how easy he or she will be to work with.

What to Discuss When You Meet Caterers

O Ask questions you may have about how they structure or price their proposals.

O Ask to see photos of events they've done to get a sense of their style.

O Discuss how your event will flow, and ask their opinion of the best way to work in your venue.

O Brainstorm about creative ways to personalize your menu.

Once you've found the caterer who fits you and your wedding best, get a contract that spells out the payment policy. Be sure it specifies cancellation policies, when your final guest count is due before the wedding, and what methods of payment they accept. Put down your deposit, and check it off your list. You will certainly make tweaks to your menu as your wedding date approaches, but the process of finding the right caterer is now out of the way.

Working with Hotel Caterers

If you've selected a venue that provides the catering, you won't need to go through the process of finding a caterer to work with. You will be assigned a catering executive or the venue's wedding specialist to guide you through the process. Although a venue's catering executive handles more things than an off-site caterer because the venue and food and sometimes even guest rooms are all wrapped up in one, don't use your contact as an ad hoc wedding planner. This goes for off-site catering execs, too.

Catering: It's Not Just Chicken Anymore

Things *Not* to Ask Your Caterer to Do

○ Give you daily advice on everything from the color of invitations to the song you should use as your first dance. Getting a list of vendor referrals is one thing; making her your personal consultant is another.

○ Run your wedding ceremony. Your caterer needs to be focused on the food and service, and she can't be doing her job if she has to spend an hour coordinating your processional.

○ Time-consuming details. If you want a bow tied on the back of each guest chair or 200 luminary bags set out along the drive to the reception, be prepared to pay for extra staff to get this done on time. These little details take tons of time, and this extra time isn't factored in to standard setup.

○ Redo your proposal every time you see an article on new catering trends.

If you need lots of extra help with details and on-site coordination, strongly consider hiring a wedding coordinator for the day. Dumping extra work and unreasonable expectations on your caterer will only create chaos. The money you think you're saving will come back to haunt you when your wedding runs late because you don't have enough staff to get the job done. Don't come back and blame me (or her) when the flow of the entire evening is off because your catering executive was busy pinning on boutonnieres while she should have been overseeing the setup.

On-Site Catering Proposals

Usually, when you book a hotel or club for your wedding, they give you a packet full of sample menus or lists of menu items. These menus are a jumping-off point and can be customized and mixed and matched to your heart's delight. Don't be afraid to ask for additional options or request that the chef customize something for your wedding. Although hotels and clubs are usually more standardized in operation, it can be done.

Most hotels and clubs offer you a package that covers the food and drinks for the entire wedding reception. The package usually includes the room rental, bar, wine with dinner, champagne toast, passed hors d'oeuvres during the cocktail hour, a two- or three-course meal (or buffet or stations), and all rentals and equipment. Because you are getting everything from them, they are able to include items in their packages that might be extras with off-site catering.

Some Extras You Might Find in a Hotel Wedding Package

○ Staging and power for your band

○ Honeymoon suite

○ Discounted parking and guest room rates

○ Wedding cake

DON'T Forget the Tax and Service Charge

In off-site catering proposals, the service is a line item and is determined by the number of waiters, bartenders, chefs, and pantry workers the catering exec thinks you'll need. In hotel and club proposals, the service is almost always a flat percentage of the overall food and beverage cost. This percentage ranges from 15 percent to more than 20 percent and is almost never included in the menu price listed on the proposal. Then on top of that, you need to add tax. In Washington, D.C., the entire food and beverage charge plus the service charge is taxed 10 percent! This means that at most luxury hotels, you're adding 30 percent on top of the menu prices. This can be quite a chunk of change, so don't forget it when computing prices.

Negotiating with Hotels

If you're getting married during an "off" season or doing a wedding reception not on a Saturday night, you might have some leeway in negotiating a better deal with your hotel. Because clubs are private and more restrictive, they usually have little leeway. But hotels want to bring in revenue, so if you're willing to do a Friday night reception or get married in the dead of winter (not around the holidays, of course) or the blistering heat of summer, there can be deals to be made.

Think through what you really need instead of what the package automatically offers. Weddings aren't one-size-fits-all, so ask for what you want instead of what they want to sell you.

Ways to Get a Better Deal with Hotels

○ Remove excess courses from the menu. Don't need soup *and* salad? Skip one course to reduce your package price.

○ Skip the dessert course, and serve wedding cake as dessert. Lots of people won't be able to eat both, anyway.

○ Skip the champagne toast if you don't think many of your guests will partake. I've seen more champagne dumped out in hotel kitchens because people don't drink it.

○ Skip the stationary hors d'oeuvres (especially when it comes to popular items such as shrimp) and just go with passed. You'll be able to control the amount served.

Just like there are smart ways to spend your money, there are unwise ways to save it. Brides often focus on the wrong things because they are so caught up in the small details and special touches that every wedding magazine convinces them are crucial to a perfect wedding. Often the unglamorous things make the most impact. Don't be so determined to save a few dollars that you make decisions that can ruin your wedding.

Things *Not* to Cut Back On

O Don't cut the wait staff. For a seated meal, you need 1 waiter per 10 to 12 guests, and for a buffet, you need at least 1 waiter per 25 guests. Fewer waiters mean less attention to your guests and dirty dishes lingering on tables longer than you'd like.

O Don't do a cash bar. Even if you must serve beer and wine only or just a few specialty alcoholic cocktails along with non-alcoholic options, that's preferable to asking your guests to fork over money for their drinks. Decide what you can afford, and do that graciously.

O Don't try to cut back on equipment or reuse items if you're at an off-site location. As crazy as it sounds, I've seen brides try it! Even though this is a big budget item in your catering proposal, be sure you have enough of everything. It is usually impractical or impossible to wash dishes for an off-site caterer.

O Don't cut back on the amount of hors d'oeuvres served. People will remember if they never saw any food during the cocktail hour.

DO Keep It Simple to Save

Don't do a choice of entrée or a duet entrée if you want to keep prices in check. Aside from being a pain in the rear end because of all the work you need to do to compile entrée choices, a choice of entrée means the caterer must have extras of all your choices because people always change their minds. Duet entrées (a beef and chicken on the same plate, for example) are also more expensive than selecting a single entrée option for everyone. Plus, you don't have to compile responses.

Catering: It's Not Just Chicken Anymore

I've found it can be easier to get things "thrown" in than to bring prices down. Catering executives are still responsible for bringing in a certain amount of money and don't always have the authority to discount their package prices substantially. If they can't bring down the package price dramatically, perhaps they are willing to offer you some extras for the same price. I've been able to get wine and bar upgrades, a complimentary wedding cake, upgraded linens or chair covers, and extra courses like a sorbet intermezzo or chocolate truffles at the end of the meal—though not all for the same wedding, mind you.

DON'T Negotiate After the Fact

Do all your negotiating before you sign a contract. Occasionally, you can get things thrown in after you've committed to the hotel, but you will have lost most of your bargaining power because they have your deposit and a signed contract. Your biggest power play is the ability to select another venue if the prices or incentives aren't good enough. Remember that this negotiating doesn't work if you're competing with 10 other brides for a top wedding hotel in June. At that point, you'd just better shut up and sign unless you don't mind losing the venue.

Moving Forward with Your Caterer

After you've selected your off-site caterer or locked in your contract with your hotel catering executive, what's next? True, you do have a little time to kick back and get some other wedding tasks done. Don't feel the need to pester your caterer for the next 6 months until your wedding just to be sure he still knows you're there, though. He hasn't forgotten you, I promise.

The next major step with your caterer will be your tasting. This is a fun time to get to sample your wedding menu, look at the tableware options, and talk about the timeline for your wedding day.

DON'T Burn Out Your Caterer

Whatever you do, don't ask for a revision of your proposal every time you think you want to change an hors d'oeuvre. Avoid this by having a good idea of what you want *before* you start getting proposals. Changing from a plated dinner to buffet and then to stations just because you don't know what you want will waste your caterer's time and force him to use your photo as a dartboard. Making changes, even small ones, takes time. Be respectful of your caterer's time, and think before you ask for a million minor changes.

Don't expect a tasting before you sign a contract. Some caterers will do it, but it is usually so early in the planning that it won't be useful. It is better to wait until you have finalized your menu and are closer to the wedding so you get the best idea of how your reception will go. If you are really worried about the quality of the food, ask to stop by an upcoming event your caterer is working to sample the food. If a caterer does do a tasting before you sign on, don't expect another one later on when you have completely changed your menu (as most people do). Tastings are more expensive to put on than you'd think, and caterers don't make enough of a profit to do multiple tastings for each client.

Another big no-no is inviting your entire wedding party or extended family to the tasting. Limit the number of people you bring to the tasting to both sets of parents and the bride and groom, if at all possible. This is a working meeting to finalize many of your wedding details, not a free dinner for 12. Do include your wedding consultant, though. Lots of details will be worked out at your tasting, so even if she doesn't eat (as I many times don't) she will want to be in the loop.

Items to Discuss at the Tasting (Aside from the Food)

○ **Flowers.** If you've selected a florist, ask him to bring a sample centerpiece so you can see it with the linens.

Catering: It's Not Just Chicken Anymore

○ **Lighting.** If you're considering special lighting for your reception, ask to have a demonstration of what it will look like. Either the hotel's in-house audio visual department will set this up or an off-site lighting company you've contacted can do a demo.

○ **Rentals.** If you're considering upgrading the linens, chairs, or tableware, now is the time to have samples sent from rental companies so you can see the overall effect with the flowers.

○ **Wedding cake.** If the hotel or caterer will be doing the cake, bring photos of cakes you like and ask to taste samples at the tasting.

○ **Wines.** It can be nice to sample some wine options with the meal. This is a good time to see if the house wine is suitable or if you'd like to consider other options. Discuss the brands of beer and liquor you want to serve, as well. Specify if you'll do champagne for just a toast, on the bar, or not at all.

Sad Story/Happy Ending

Despite my advice (and the caterer's) that she wait, one bride insisted on doing a tasting very early on in the planning. She treated it more like a party than a productive meeting because she hadn't gotten far enough in the planning to know what questions would be important later. Of course, 6 months later she regretted her decision and wanted another tasting because she didn't remember a thing about the first one and had changed her mind on everything regarding the food. I had to beg the caterer to do another tasting, which he agreed to after a lot of grumbling. Although everything worked out, the bride was embarrassed that she hadn't listened to our professional advice.

After you've done your tasting and finalized every detail of the food, you just need to keep the lines of communication open with your caterer leading up to your wedding day. If you want to donate leftovers to charity or have the staff prepare a "to go" basket for you at the end of the night, let your caterer know ahead of time.

Catering Details to Remember

○ **The final guest count.** Usually this is due a few days before the event, but check your contract so you don't get stuck paying for extra guests because you didn't give the guest count on time.

○ **Any changes in the timing or location of the event.** You'd be shocked at how many brides change the time of their wedding and never inform the caterer!

○ **Your floor plan.** This includes the number of tables and how many guests are seated at each one. Be sure to include where kids and vegetarians are seated, as well as any guests in wheelchairs.

○ **Meal breakdown.** If you have a choice of entrée, your caterer needs this breakdown by table and entrée, as well as how you will indicate the choice for the waiters.

To get the most from your caterer, whether off-site or on-site, you should do your homework and be prepared. Know what you want before you start shopping around, but also be open to creative suggestions and ways to save. Understanding what makes the biggest impact and what guests will hardly miss can be the difference between a successful wedding and a near disaster.

Catering

Do	Don't
✓ Know what you want before you call caterers.	✗ Get too many catering proposals.
✓ See if your hotel will throw in some extras.	✗ Treat your caterer like a wedding consultant.
✓ Forget to give your caterer important information.	✗ Schedule your tasting too early.

7

Come One, Come All

One of the elements of wedding planning that seems to take on a life of its own is the guest list. If you aren't careful, it can expand at a rate that makes the Blob look like child's play. The key to controlling the madness is knowing how to set limits and keep the list in check from the beginning. In this chapter, I help you tame that wild beast. You also learn how to take care of your guests before they even arrive.

How to Set Limits

Before you start enthusiastically inviting everyone you've ever met, you need to have a serious talk with all the involved parties about the guest list. This means both sets of parents (or multiple sets in the case of divorced parents) and you and your fiancé need to be on the same page from the start.

Mistakes That Spin Your Guest List Out of Control

○ Inviting a date for every single guest.

○ Inviting families with all their children (especially if you don't know the kids).

○ Turning your wedding into a career networking event for your parents or future in-laws.

○ Thinking you must invite everyone in your office.

Your guest list may be limited by your budget or the size of your venue or just by the fact that you would like a smaller wedding, but every list needs to have a set limit. Once you have decided on the total guest count, give each side of the family (or set of parents) their allotted number, and tell them to stick to it. One common way of dividing the list is to split the total guest limit into four and give one fourth each to the bride's parents, the groom's parents, the bride, and the groom. You may choose to split things up differently, of course, but however you work things out, be sure to set a limit early.

One of the most common mistakes regarding the guest list is assuming that enough people will decline that you can invite many more than you intend to have at the reception. True, some of your guests won't be able to attend, but it's a total crapshoot as to how many. I've seen the percentage range from a high 20 percent when lots of guests were from out of town to a low 5 percent when almost all the guests were local. Don't invite an extra 50 guests and assume you'll get a high enough drop-out rate to hit your target guest count. You might find yourself over budget and bursting out of your venue. If you must factor in an attrition rate, be on the safe side and stick with 10 percent.

Sad Story/Happy Ending

The mother of one of my brides was so out of control with her guest list that she invited almost 100 more guests than would fit in the hotel ballroom. Despite pleas from me and the hotel catering manager, she ended up with so many guests that people were wedged into tables shoulder to shoulder. We were lucky that the fire marshal didn't pop by for a visit, because we were over the legal room capacity as well! Fortunately, the guests were very easygoing (not all would have been), and we moved tables as soon as dinner ended and people started dancing so there would be more room to move. Everything turned out okay and people had a great time, but the hotel catering manager and I nearly got ulcers because of it.

Come One, Come All

Wedding Reception or Meat Market?

Beware of the many insidious ways your guest list can grow beyond your wildest dreams, and establish rules early on. One of the biggest questions I get is regarding dates to weddings. I'm a believer that a wedding is a personal event where you should be surrounded by those people who are nearest and dearest to you, not by your cousin's latest hook-up. There are exceptions to my "no date" stance, of course.

When to Invite Dates

○ The couple is engaged.

○ The couple is living together.

○ The couple has been dating exclusively for many months.

○ Your maid of honor wants to bring a date.

It can be tough to draw the line, but if you don't, you'll find your wedding is full of people you've never met and will most likely never lay eyes on again. One additional exception to the rule extends to the wedding party. I have many brides who allow their bridesmaids and groomsmen to invite dates as a small reward for being forced into chartreuse satin and rented shoes. I think this is a fair allowance. Considering some of the bridesmaids' dresses I've seen, they should be allowed to bring a dozen dates.

Send in the Clowns ... and Baby-Sitters

Another sticky topic is children. People get very touchy about being asked to leave their kids behind. I've seen families stop speaking to each other because of this issue! I've always thought parents would jump at the chance to have a night out without their children, but not all feel this way. If you have decided to have an adult-only reception, make that clear early on. Although you shouldn't put anything on your invitation that references children (putting "adults only" or "adult reception" on your formal invitation is a big etiquette no-no), spread the word early and often in other ways.

71

Ways to Ward Off Children

○ Include the fact that the wedding will be an adult-only reception in your save-the-date mailing and all follow-up mailings (except on the actual invitation).

○ Have your family and bridal party spread the word. Sometimes it's easier for your mother to tell her family members directly and soften the blow.

○ Provide baby-sitting options. Either hire sitters to be at the reception site (in a separate room) and handle the children on-site, or provide the names of qualified sitters for parents to have come to their hotel rooms.

○ Set up a separate kid's reception near to but out of sight of the wedding reception. Provide kids' meals, entertainment, favors, and sitters to supervise.

Be creative with kids, and the parents will love you forever. Even if you will have children attending your reception, have some ways to keep them amused so they don't start tearing around the room. Favor bags full of coloring books and crayons, silent and nonhazardous toys, and candy that won't stain and get on everything will keep kids occupied. Or you can set up separate craft stations where children can work on projects with adult supervision.

DO Be Consistent

If you have decided not to invite any children under 12, stick to that plan. Once you start bending the rules, feelings will get hurt and people will be resentful that someone else's child was allowed to come and theirs weren't. If you are consistent, no one can accuse you of being unfair.

Keeping the List

You can keep your guest list in many ways, from wedding software to a legal pad of paper. I recommend using some kind of computer program, whether it's a customized program for wedding guest lists or just a spreadsheet that can be downloaded into a Word file.

It's important to be able to convert your guest list into an easy-to-read "stacked" list of names. By *stacked,* I mean typed out as it would look on the invitation with the name on top and the address lines directly below. Many hand calligraphers refuse to read off a spreadsheet because it makes them cross-eyed.

DO **Check the Format**

Before you send off your guest list to the calligrapher (hand calligraphers and machine calligraphers), check that you have it in the proper format. Having to re-type your list after the fact will be a huge waste of time and might just push you over the edge.

There are lots of etiquette rules on the proper addressing of invitations. In fact, entire books have been written on the subject, which is why I'm not going to go into the zillion combinations in this book. If you have numerous tricky addressing situations, check out *Crane's Wedding Blue Book* (Simon & Schuster, 1993) for the absolute final word on perfect etiquette.

Simple Invitation-Addressing Rules

○ Include the names of dates and children. Try to avoid the phrases "and guest" or "and family."

- Don't abbreviate. Spell out everything in the addresses, including states and words such as *Street, Boulevard, Suite,* and *Drive.*

- Double-check titles. If a guest is a doctor of English literature, be sure to address him as Doctor. If his wife is also a doctor, don't call her Mrs.

DO Start Early

Begin compiling and confirming addresses as soon as you start your guest list (and be sure your fiancé and parents are doing the same). Often a few straggling addresses hold up sending the list off to the calligrapher.

Taking Care of Your Guests

Well, they made it on the list. Now it's time to make some preparations for your guests. A considerate bride understands that for out-of-town guests, traveling to your wedding can be a major expense and undertaking. Do everything possible to make their trip an easy and enjoyable one.

Getting Them There

Unless most of your guests are local or within driving distance of your wedding, you will have some guests who will be arriving via plane or train. It is helpful to give them as much information as possible ahead of time.

Ways to Make Travel Easier for Your Guests

- Get a wedding discount for your guests who use certain airlines. American Airlines has a great program that includes discounts on rental cars.

○ Provide directions from the airport or train station to the hotels you recommend.

○ Provide approximate cab fares from the airports and train stations and how long it will take to get there.

○ Arrange for family and friends to pick up arriving guests and take them to their hotels.

If a lot of your guests will be driving in, it is nice to provide directions from major highways to the hotels and any insider driving tips. Also, let them know how much it will cost to park their cars at the hotels.

Hotels

One of the more tedious wedding-planning tasks (in my humble opinion) is booking blocks of guest rooms at hotels. This is something to get out of the way early so eager-beaver guests can go ahead and make their reservations. I promise you, if you don't do it soon, your mother will start calling you every day to ask if you've done it yet.

To book a block of rooms, call around to several hotels in the vicinity of your wedding and get rates and availability. Be sure to specify that you want a block for a wedding and ask if there's an attrition clause in their room-block contract. If there is, ask to have it removed in exchange for having the rooms released back to the hotel 3 weeks to a month prior to the wedding. Hotels are usually fine with blocking rooms without a financial commitment from you if they can be assured that they can rent them out to the general public if your group doesn't book them.

Items to Look for in a Room-Block Contract

○ **Attrition rate.** You do not want one of these clauses that penalizes you for any rooms not booked. These are common in corporate contracts but should not be in social ones.

- ○ **The cutoff date.** This is the date the rooms will be released back into general reservations. Be sure to tell your guests to call before this date or they won't get the special rate—or possibly any room at all.

- ○ **Individual call-in and pay.** This specifies that the guests will be paying for their own rooms and making their own reservations, not you.

- ○ **The number of rooms blocked per night, the price, and the types of rooms.** Be sure to spell out how many rooms of each type (king bed or two doubles) you want each night.

I usually recommend getting three hotel options for your guests. One should be your "hub" hotel. This hotel should be convenient and priced reasonably enough for most of your guests to be able to stay there. Then you may want to offer a lower-priced option. This might not be as close to the action as the hub hotel but is great for friends right out of school who want to keep costs down and stack themselves in like sardines. Finally, you may have a need for a higher-priced option. Maybe your parents' friends would prefer to be at a luxury hotel away from all the wedding hustle and bustle. List all these options with phone numbers, cutoff dates, and pricing on all mailings and your wedding website.

Welcoming Touches

Beyond providing the basic information on travel and hotels, you can make your guests' stay a memorable one in other ways as well. It's becoming more and more common to provide welcome bags or welcoming information for your out-of-town guests. These bags can be simple ways to be sure your guests have all the times and directions, or they can be lavish gifts of food and keepsakes. Most brides offer something in the middle.

Items to Include in Your Welcome Bags

○ A welcome note from the bride and groom

○ An itinerary of the weekend's events

○ Maps and directions to all wedding locations

○ Timing and pick-up locations for any transportation provided

After providing the essential information, the personal details are up to you. Keep in mind that you might need to do 50 or 60 or more of these bags, so it can be easy to spend hundreds or even thousands of dollars on these. Remember that the little things add up quickly!

Be willing to get creative with your welcome bags. Use unusual containers such as metal boxes or miniature paint buckets. (I ransack The Container Store and The Home Depot regularly looking for ideas.) Think of ways to personalize your gifts with favorite foods and details about your wedding or locale. Don't feel like you have to spend a lot to make your welcome bags memorable. The fact that you provide them will stick in your guests' minds more.

Creative, Low-Cost Welcome Bag Ideas

○ A "Top Ten" list of the bride and groom's favorite places of interest or local restaurants.

○ A recipe for the groom's favorite cookies and a small bag of the homemade cookies.

○ Local postcards of the area serve as an inexpensive keepsake.

○ Miniature bags of favorite candies or nibbles. Or buy in bulk and repackage in small bags or tins.

DON'T Forget the Logistics

Figure out how you will get 60 large gift baskets to the hotels before your living room floor is covered from end to end and only about 10 will fit in your car. Also think about the logistics of how your guests will get heavy or cumbersome welcome gifts home in a suitcase. Don't spend tons of money on things that will get left behind in the hotels.

Being a good hostess doesn't mean paying for everyone's hotel rooms or arranging elaborate tours once everyone is in town (although that would certainly be memorable). It just means taking the time to think about your guests and what will make getting to and attending your wedding easy and enjoyable. Providing information and helpful tips tells your guests you care about them enough to go to the trouble and makes you a stand-out bride.

The Guest List and the Guests

Do	Don't
✓ Be consistent with your guest list rules.	✗ Count on lots of no-shows.
✓ Start confirming addresses early.	✗ Use abbreviations in addresses.
✓ Provide transportation and hotel information early.	✗ Get stuck with a hotel attrition clause.

8

You Are Invited: Demystifying Invitations

So what is really important anymore when it comes to invitations? In this chapter, I walk you through the minefield of printing styles and invitation components and let you in on what is worth the money and what is better left behind. Then I give you the skinny on how to word your invitations so everyone is happy.

To Engrave or Not to Engrave?

One of the first decisions you need to make regarding the printed matter for your wedding is how you want it all printed. This goes hand-in-hand with deciding how much you want to spend on invitations and the like. If you've always envisioned heavy Crane's cards engraved with your monogram, then set aside a chunk of change in your budget. If, however, invitations come low down on your wedding priority totem pole, going with a less expensive option makes much more sense.

Engraving

Engraving is the classic printing method in which a metal plate is made with your invitation wording and each invitation is actually engraved from this plate. It is one of the more costly and time-consuming printing methods, but it provides a timeless look that is always elegant. The style options for engraved invitations have remained constant for the most part, so some of the colorful and creative options you might have seen won't be available through classic engraving companies. Also, remember that engraving is not a rush job, so you should allow at least 6 weeks to have invitations printed.

Thermography

Thermography is the printing method that comes closest to the look of engraving, but at a fraction of the cost. Instead of the text being engraved into the paper, powder is sprinkled onto ink and raised letters are formed. The look is almost identical to engraving with differences only a practiced eye can spot. One big advantage to thermography is the turnaround time. Invitations can be printed in a matter of days instead of the many weeks engraving requires.

Differences Between Engraving and Thermography

- Thermography does not have the slight indentations on the back of the card like an engraved invitation.

- Thermography ink is slightly shinier than engraved ink, which is more matte.

- Thermography costs about half of what engraving does.

- Thermography takes a fraction of the turnaround time engraving does.

I've found that the quality and weight of the paper is more important than the printing method. I'd much rather see a thermography invitation on a heavy, all-cotton paper than an engraved invitation on a thin, flimsy, wood-pulp card. People will instinctively notice the weight and feel of the paper more than they'll notice the faint indentations on the back. So if you're torn between thermography and engraving, put your money in the paper first.

Letterpress

Letterpress is an old printing method that has recently seen a huge resurgence in popularity. It is similar to engraving in the length of time it requires (at least 6 weeks and often more) and the fact that the text is actually pressed into the paper. Letterpress doesn't require a metal plate like engraving does, though. The look of letterpress invitations is quite different from engraving as well. The paper is usually more heavily textured (it almost looks like it was handmade), and the overall effect is much softer and less crisp than engraved print.

One more thing to note: letterpress costs about the same as engraving, so although the look is soft and a bit less formal, the price is not.

Flat Printing

Flat printing, or offset printing, is pretty much what it sounds like: flat, printed ink that is not raised from the page. The paper is completely flat on both sides, and the ink is usually matte. This method is best used for other invitation components and not the actual invitation because it is less formal and has less impact. There are exceptions to this rule, of course. Some very modern invitations require flat printing because of their design, and some very intricate lettering is better done in flat printing than engraving or thermography so the detail will show. Flat printing is perfect for invitations that require printing on both sides and for direction cards with maps on the reverse. The cost for flat printing is the lowest of all the options.

Save the Date!

Chances are, before your guests receive the formal invitation to your wedding, they will have already received a save-the-date card or a packet of travel information. Many brides today send some kind of early notice to let friends and family know the date and location of the wedding several months in advance. This is a great idea, given most people's hectic and busy schedules. This way they can be sure to mark the date on their calendars. Plan to mail these 4 to 8 months before the wedding, but avoid mailing around holidays, or it will get lost in the shuffle.

Save-the-dates can be anything from a simple postcard to an elaborate booklet with numerous pages of information. Don't feel the need to get these engraved or letterpressed to match your invitation (unless you have money to burn). This is a place where creativity is more important than formality. I even had one bride have her kindergarten class draw a picture of a bride and groom for her save-the-date. Have fun, and let your personality show!

Must-Include Save-the-Date Card Information

○ The wedding date

○ Your names (first and last)

○ The location of the wedding (at least the city and state)

○ An indication that a formal invitation will follow (You'd be shocked by how many people get confused and think this is the invitation.)

Once you've included the basic information, you can add as much or as little as you want. Many clients include their personal wedding website address so people can go to that for more details. Others also include the basic hotel and airline contact information so guests can book early. The most industrious brides prepare entire booklets of tourist tips and area activities. This more detailed information can also be sent much later to only the guests you know will attend or can be tucked into the welcome bags you take to the hotels.

The Invitation Components: What You Need and What You Don't

Aside from the actual invitation, most brides need one or more separate enclosures. Some of these are practical and essential, and some are a colossal waste of money. Don't feel forced to include half a dozen enclosures in your invitation. Nothing ruins the look of a beautiful invitation more than a huge stack of enclosures and envelopes falling out of the envelope.

Most brides can survive with just a reception card, a response card, and the envelope set. Rarely do I see weddings that require pew cards or transportation cards. Don't do tons of enclosures just for the sake of doing them, and don't let a stationery store try to sell you things you don't absolutely need.

Ways to Save on Invitation Enclosures

○ Put the reception information on your invitation, and skip the reception card. This only works well if your invitation is larger than the standard 5x7 card.

○ Throw caution to the wind and don't do a response card. This means you expect people to know they must write their responses to you on their own stationery, which almost none do. This might cause more headaches than it's worth.

○ Print maps and directions yourself in a coordinating paper.

○ Skip envelope liners and other extras.

Wording Invitations

Nothing can cause as much anxiety as trying to word your invitations if you have a complicated or sticky family situation. Tradition dictates certain rules for various situations, but I've found that sometimes you have to break with tradition to keep families happy.

The traditional wording of an invitation is as follows:

Mr. and Mrs. John Doe
request the honour of your presence
at the marriage of their daughter
Jane Elizabeth
to
John Franklin Jones
Saturday, the fourth of June
Two thousand and five
at five o'clock,
St. John's Episcopal Church
Washington, District of Columbia

Note: The British spelling of *honour* is used most often in wedding invitations and in *Crane's Wedding Blue Book,* but either spelling is acceptable.

DON'T Abbreviate

Remember to spell out everything on a wedding invitation, from your full names (even if you hate your middle name) to the state your wedding will be held in. Mr., Mrs., Ms., and Jr. are abbreviated, though.

Inviting Guests Yourself

It is appropriate to have an invitation issued from the bride and groom if you are the ones paying for the wedding and your families aren't very involved. You may also want to do the inviting if your families are so complicated that to include everyone's name would take up so much of the invitation there would be no room for anything else. It can be a great way to be inclusive and avoid hurting feelings. But if one or both families are contributing to the wedding and are involved, be sure to run this option by them first. They might feel excluded.

You Are Invited: Demystifying Invitations

Here are a few ways to word the invitation:

Jane Elizabeth Doe
and
John Franklin Jones
request the honour of your presence
at their marriage

Or:

The honour of your presence
is requested at the marriage of
Jane Elizabeth Doe
and
John Franklin Jones

DO Know the Difference

When a ceremony takes place in a religious house of worship, the phrase "the honour of your presence" is traditionally used on the invitation. When the ceremony takes place outside a religious setting (even when presided over by a priest or rabbi), the phrase "the pleasure of your company" is used. If you are having a black-tie wedding outside a church or synagogue, however, you may feel that "the pleasure of your company" isn't formal enough, in which case you should use the wording that matches the formality of the event (even if it isn't painfully proper).

Including Both Sets of Parents

More and more often, the groom's family is being included on the invitation, either because they're contributing to the wedding or just because the bride and groom want both families to be equally acknowledged. This is traditionally done for more conservative Jewish weddings.

Here's how to word the invitation:

Mr. and Mrs. John Doe
Mr. and Mrs. Roger Jones
request the honour of your presence
at the marriage of their daughter
Jane Elizabeth
to
John Franklin Jones

Or:

Mr. and Mrs. John Doe
request the honour of your presence
at the marriage of their daughter
Jane Elizabeth
to
John Franklin Jones,
son of Mr. and Mrs. Roger Jones

Including Divorced and Remarried Parents

Okay, here's where it gets tricky. If your parents are divorced, their names go one after the other at the top of the invitation:

Mrs. Catherine Doe
Mr. Howard Doe
request the honour of your presence
at the marriage of their daughter
Jane Elizabeth
to
Mr. John Franklin Jones

If there are two sets of remarried parents, the couples' names should be stacked on top of each other at the top of the invitation. The bride's mother always goes before the father. (Or save yourself the headache and go with an invitation issued by the bride and groom, as mentioned earlier.)

Mr. and Mrs. Andrew Simon Smith
Mr. and Mrs. Howard Joseph Doe
request the honour of your presence
at the marriage of their daughter
Jane Elizabeth
to
Mr. John Franklin Jones

There are so many permutations for wording wedding invitations that I highly recommend getting a copy of *Crane's Wedding Blue Book*. Not only will it help you word your invitations and know how to address your envelopes, but you will find yourself referring to it long after your wedding is over.

Ordering Invitations

You've picked an invitation, a printing style, and even finalized the wording. Now for some nitty-gritty on ordering your invitations and stationery. First off, allow plenty of time for the proofing and printing process. Even if the stationery store says the company can print them in a week, you need to factor in the time for getting and approving a proof. Don't forget shipping time or time that it might take to redo invitations if they're wrong or get damaged in route.

Always do a careful count of your guest list before ordering invitations. A general guideline for ordering the right number of invitations is to take your guest count and divide it in half, and then add 25 to 50. Remember that you are ordering one invitation per household, not per guest! This method is not precise, though, so always count before you order, or you may find yourself placing expensive reorders later. It's not cheap to order a small batch of invitations after the fact. Order at least 25 more invitations than you think you'll need and about 15 percent more envelopes than invitations. That way, when you goof up on an address, it won't be the end of the world.

DON'T Skip the Proof

Unless you are so crunched for time that an extra 48 hours will make or break you, always ask for a proof. So many mistakes are caught at this stage that it scares me to think of breezing past this part. Often a bride will change her mind on type-style once she sees it in print, as well. It is much better to take the time to see a proof and check over it carefully than to have to pay for a reorder.

Print the return address in a font that matches your invitation or the calligraphy style you choose for addressing (or if you like to be very traditional, you can blind emboss). Traditionally, the hosts of the wedding receive the response cards and have their name on the back of the invitation envelope. I must admit that many of my brides just don't want the hassle of having to get daily updates from parents, or have parents who might not be up to the task. For practicality, I just look the other way and hope the etiquette gods don't strike me down.

Sad Story/Happy Ending

Whatever you do, don't include a line on your response card for the number of guests attending. A former bride insisted on this line on her response card (despite my many warnings) and then was shocked when she got many cards with additional guests written in. Luckily she had enough space in her ballroom to accommodate the add-ons (and budget wasn't a big concern), but not all brides would have been so lucky.

The Finishing Touches

You have your invitations in your hands. Now the wedding seems real, doesn't it? Take a few moments to consider the impact of the arriving invitation when you select addressing methods and postage. These may seem like afterthoughts, but they are the first things a guest will see. I'll never forget an invitation I received years ago that was addressed in what looked like green magic marker and had mismatched stamps on it. It stuck out because it made such a bad impression.

Calligraphy: By Hand or Machine

There's nothing quite like the beauty of hand-calligraphy—or the expense! If having spectacular envelopes is one of your wedding priorities, then go for it. If invitations aren't high on your priority list, then I'm betting spending between $2 and $6 per invitation to have them hand-calligraphied isn't in the budget.

Alternatives to Expensive Hand-Calligraphy

- ○ Write them out yourself (if you have nice handwriting).

- ○ Beg your mother or a bridesmaid to help you if your handwriting resembles chicken scratch.

- ○ Consider machine calligraphy. Professional computer calligraphy is so pretty that it can be mistaken for the real deal. And it costs a fraction of what hand-calligraphy does.

- ○ Have the same company that prints your invitations do the addressing. Some companies offer this machine calligraphy service and will print them in the same font and exact ink color of your invitation. The great part about this is that you receive the envelopes already addressed and ready to mail!

Under pain of death, don't print out labels on your computer and stick them on your formal wedding invitations. There's no quicker way to cheapen your invitation than to give it a computerized label, no matter how nice the font is. My eye starts to twitch just thinking about this horror!

Stuffing and Mailing

Before you rush off to the post office, take a few moments to prepare and stuff your invitations properly. If your invitation comes with tissue, place that directly on top of the invitation (touching the ink). Then stack the other enclosures in ascending size order (biggest card on the bottom) and tuck all of them inside your fold-over invitation or on top of your invitation if it is a card. All this goes in your inner envelope (if your invitation comes with one), which gets tucked (unsealed) into the main envelope so the name written on the inner envelope shows as the guest pulls it out.

DO **Try This Trick**

Make a numbered, alphabetical list of everyone invited to the wedding. Then, as you're stuffing the invitations, write the guest's number on the back of the response card in pencil. This way if a guest forgets to write their name on the card (and this happens all the time), you won't be stuck trying to guess who they are.

Mail invitations between 4 to 8 weeks before the wedding. If you have invitations going overseas, you may send these out at 10 weeks to give ample time. It is a good idea to take a sample invitation with all the enclosures to the post office and have it weighed before you buy stamps. Oversized invitations take more postage, and extras such as enclosures and envelope liners increase the overall weight. Remember to buy stamps for the response card envelope and prestamp them (unless they're going overseas—in which case, don't bother).

You Are Invited: Demystifying Invitations

If you can get your post office to hand-cancel your invitations, by all means go for it (or offer to do the stamping yourself). It will create less wear and tear on your invitations. Post offices are less than thrilled to hand-cancel 200 invitations, but a little begging never hurt.

Invitations

Do	Don't
✓ Consider the cost and timing of your printing options.	✗ Order enclosures you don't need.
✓ Send save-the-date cards so guests can mark their calendars.	✗ Think your save-the-date cards must match your invitations.
✓ Be careful when wording your invitations.	✗ Follow strict etiquette rules if they will cause hurt feelings.

9

To Give and to Receive

Admit it. One of the best things about getting married is the gifts. Registering for gifts is one of the secret guilty pleasures of engaged women. This is one of the few times in your life when you will get to select ridiculously priced gifts and people will gladly run out and buy them for you. Don't get so sucked into the "gimme-gimme" syndrome that you forget to show appreciation, though. In this chapter, not only do you learn how to properly thank your attendants and guests, but you find out how to avoid going too far into the wedding gift game.

Put Down the Registry Gun!

Before you rush out in a delirious shopping frenzy to register at your 10 favorite stores, stop and take a few moments to think about what you really need for your lifestyle. The whole point of a registry is to get items that will suit your current life, not a life you aspire to in 20 years. Registering for a closet full of formal china you will never use is just bad shopping strategy.

Questions to Ask Yourself Before You Register

- ○ Do you entertain often? Casually or formally?
- ○ Do you cook? Be honest. No sense getting pricey pans if you live on take-out.

○ How large is your house or apartment, and how much storage space does it have? If you get crates of china you'll store for later use, be sure you have someplace to put it.

○ Will you be inheriting any china or crystal?

After you've given your lifestyle an honest appraisal, you're more prepared to select registry gifts that will reflect you as a couple and be practical for your married life. Remember, you don't have to stick with the traditional housewares when you register. If you're a nature-loving couple, you might be more inclined to sign up for camping gear than Waterford champagne flutes.

Share the Wealth

Unless you live in an area that only has one decent store to register in, it makes sense to select a few different places to set up a wedding registry. This gives options for guests who may live all over the country and also gives your wish list some variety. I don't mean you should register at three department stores and half a dozen specialty stores— that's overkill.

Your wedding registries should complement and balance each other. Don't register for your casual china at three different stores unless you want to invest a lot of time after the wedding making returns. Many of my clients register at a major department store, a specialty store for kitchen and casual items, and a home store for tools and more groom-friendly items.

As with everything in wedding planning, you need to be sure this plan works for you. You might instead decide to register at two different department stores to accommodate family and friends from different regions of the country and no specialty stores at all. If it works for you and your guests, go for it! Don't forget that there are many options aside from the traditional registries, and a favorite store might be willing to set one up for you even if it doesn't have an established program.

Creative Registry Alternatives

○ Museum stores and galleries

○ Bookstores and music stores

○ Wine stores

○ Craft and hobby shops

○ Travel agent (for your honeymoon)

○ Garden stores or nurseries

Ready, Set, Register!

You've decided what types of gifts will suit your lifestyle and narrowed down your store options. Now for the fun (and sometimes) hard part: the actual registering. Call ahead and ask if you need to make an appointment. Try to make an appointment during the week instead of on the weekend. You'll get more attention and better service when the store isn't crazed with shoppers and other brides with the same idea. Dress comfortably, and be prepared to stay for a while. You'd be shocked at the lengthy discussions you and your fiancé will get into over towel colors.

You might not make all your final decisions the first time you venture out. Don't worry if you need to break up the process over several weeks. Registering can be an exhausting task and can leave you with frayed nerves, so pace yourself.

How to Make a Good Registry List

○ Select gifts in a wide range of prices.

○ Give enough variety in the low-, medium-, and high-price ranges, or those few items in the lower range will be snapped up.

○ Don't select patterns that are so expensive you will only receive a few odd pieces.

○ Don't shy away from the unglamorous and practical gifts like kitchen scissors or toilet brushes. Sometimes these are the ones you'll use the most.

Sad Story/Happy Ending

If you have the inkling that your fiancé might not be warmed by the thought of spending an afternoon picking out tablecloths and duvets, try to go to the stores by yourself first and narrow down your top picks. One of my brides envisioned a joyful afternoon of merrily skipping through the aisles of the department stores with her beloved and was shocked to find that he was restless and grumpy after about an hour. She called me in tears, and I had to explain to her the valuable concept of preshopping. She returned to the store solo and selected all her favorites and then brought her fiancé back several weeks later for his approval. This time the process went much faster, and there wasn't even time for him to get restless.

Going High Tech

The Internet has revolutionized the world of wedding registries over the past few years. Even if you sign up with brick-and-mortar stores, your registry will almost always be available online. This is helpful to guests who may live nowhere near the stores you've registered in or to guests who prefer to do their shopping while they surf.

If you choose to register entirely online, try to visit a store to see items in person before signing up online. If that isn't a possibility, be sure to check out photos and confirm that the store has a liberal return policy if the item looks totally different than you expected. Even if you don't sign up online, the web is the easiest way to keep track of your registries and update them as needed. It is so much easier to hop online to see if you need to add more options than it is to drive to a department store. Of course, a trip to the mall is always a good excuse for a new pair of shoes ....

DO Ask About Store Policies

Always know how a store's return and exchange policies work before signing on with an online site or traditional store. Does the store offer a discount policy for you to complete your patterns after the wedding? How long will your registry stay online or available to guests? These aren't things to find out the hard way.

Keep It Quiet

After spending all that time and energy creating the perfect registries at just the right number of stores, you might be tempted to take out a billboard on the highway. Fight the urge. You should never make any sort of announcement concerning your registries. This includes save-the-dates, invitations, and websites. If a department store offers to give you cute preprinted inserts or send e-mails to your guests, just say no!

The only appropriate way to spread the word about your registries is through the grapevine. If someone asks, then by all means tell them. You may authorize your immediate families and attendants to tell inquiring guests, as well. The key word here is *discretion*. No one should ever offer the information before they have been asked. Never, under any circumstances, mention that you'd prefer cash or put that anywhere on your invitations. I get cold chills just thinking about it.

A Million Thanks

The most common bad bride behavior is unwritten and neglected thank you notes. Whatever you do, don't comfort yourself with the old adage that it's better late than never. A gift should not go more than 6 weeks without a handwritten response (2 months at most if you take a long honeymoon). Neglecting to send thank you notes promptly will leave your guests with a bad memory, regardless of how fabulous your wedding was.

Ways to Keep Up with Thank Yous

○ Keep very good records of the gifts you receive. As soon as something arrives, make a note of the gift, the giver, and the date it arrived. Keep track of when you mail each thank you note.

○ Respond to prewedding gifts as they come in. It is so much easier than waiting until they pile up after the wedding.

○ Let your fiancé write the notes to his family and friends.

○ Divide and conquer. If you have a huge stack of thank you notes to write, break them into groups of fives or tens and do that many each night.

It may seem impossible that you'll be able to come up with dozens and even hundreds of personal and creative thank you notes. Keep in mind that these do not have to be Nobel Prize–winning works of literature. Notes can be short, as long as they are personal. Be sure to mention the gift and how you will use it, or in the case of cash, how you will spend it. Don't obsess over grammar or finding the perfect word, or you'll be celebrating your silver wedding anniversary before you finish writing all of them.

DON'T Think You've Found a Loophole

Just because you may have thanked someone in person or over the phone doesn't mean you're absolved of your duty to write a thank you note. Nice try, though.

Shower Power

Chances are good that you'll have at least one bridal shower during your engagement. Thankfully, showers have evolved from the days of cheesy games where someone ended up wrapped in toilet paper to sophisticated soirées.

Bridal Shower Rules

○ Showers should not be thrown by relatives.

○ If someone is invited to the shower, they should be on the wedding guest list. The only exception is a work shower.

○ Don't invite people to more than one shower (the exceptions to this rule are the mothers, sisters, and bridesmaids).

○ Don't include registry information in the invitation.

How Many Is Too Many?

Although at first glance the thought of several showers may sound like a great idea (what could be bad about more presents, right?), consider wisely. Although having multiple showers is sometimes the only solution to families and friends who are spread out, they can be tiring and time-consuming. Do you really want to spend every other weekend in the months leading up to your wedding at a different shower?

If you do have more than one shower, try to limit the number of showers in one area. Even if it means mixing groups of friends, you'll save yourself headaches and your friends will save money by combining efforts. When you do have many showers, be sure to cross reference the lists so guests aren't invited to multiple showers. Bridesmaids are the exception. But if they do attend more than one shower, they shouldn't get you more than one shower gift.

Themes That Aren't Tired

Although bridal showers traditionally were about as much fun as watching paint dry, there are ways to make them more appealing.

First of all, skip the games. Second, consider changing the format. Who said showers have to be afternoon parties? Why not try a couple's shower so the guys won't miss out on all the fun, or an evening cocktail party, or even a casual cookout or pool party?

Surviving the Shower with Style

Getting showered with gifts is hardly considered a tough job, but you can still make yourself stand out as a gracious bride. The shower is good practice for the social skills you will need on your wedding day.

Here are some tips for handling bridal showers:

- Mingle with all the guests, not just your close friends and bridesmaids.

- Arrive at the time your hostess asks you to.

- Go along with the party plan, even if it includes a game of "toilet paper bride."

- Thank each guest for coming, and be effusive as you open gifts.

Wedding Party Gifts They Won't Toss

You've asked them to travel halfway across the country and shell out $200 for a taffeta bridesmaid dress that will never again see the light of day, or wear the world's most uncomfortable rented tuxedo shoes. If any people deserve appreciation, it is your wedding party. To thank them, you can present them with gifts at the rehearsal dinner or at separate events such as the bridesmaids' luncheon—always with a personal note, of course.

Take a few moments to think about each person you're shopping for. This helps you select a gift that is unique to them and memorable.

How to Select Personalized Gifts for Your Wedding Party

❍ What are the person's hobbies and interests?

❍ Is the person a wine buff or foodie?

❍ What types of books, movies, and music does he or she enjoy?

❍ Does he or she collect anything?

Gifts "Maid" to Order

Before you rush out to buy matching sets of jewelry for your bridal attendants, stop and consider your attendants. It might be nicer to give them a gift that isn't related to the wedding day. This way the gift is more about them than about your desire for them to match.

It is no longer required to give each girl the exact same gift, either. As a matter of fact, it can be very thoughtful to give gifts that fit each of your bridesmaids' unique personalities.

Unique Bridesmaid's Gifts

❍ Spa baskets with gift certificates for treatments

❍ Personalized stationery

❍ Makeup bags filled with goodies

❍ Pashminas or evening wraps

Toys for the Boys

Grooms sometimes get stuck when they try to think up the perfect gift for their friends. Brides are eager to steer them in the direction of the money clips and other nondescript mementos, but why not personalize their gifts as well? And by personalize, I don't mean monogram.

Creative Groomsmen's Gifts

O Tickets to sporting events

O Tool boxes or Swiss Army knives (fancy ones)

O Electronic organizers or mp3 players

O A box of cigars

O Satellite radio

Saying thank you with a well-thought-out gift shows your attendants how important they are to you and how much it means to you that they are part of your wedding day. Of course, it is nice if you also mention these things in the note you attach to the gift.

DON'T Forget the Little People

It's nice to give small mementos to your children attendants. Lockets are lovely for little girls, and games (electronic or not) are big hits with boys.

Receiving and Giving Gifts

Do	Don't
✓ Register for gifts that fit your lifestyle.	✗ Register for items with too little variety in price.
✓ Write thank you notes promptly.	✗ Have family members throw you a shower.
✓ Personalize your attendant gifts.	✗ Invite guests to a shower but not to the wedding.

10

Looking the Part

Your wedding dress is likely to be the single most expensive item of clothing you'll ever buy. Nothing transforms a price tag quite so magically as the words *wedding gown* or makes a bride quite so nutty. Even my most casual Birkenstock brides get swept away in the search for the perfect dress. And what dress would be complete without the perfect veil, shoes, tiara, gloves, hair ...? Well, you get the picture. In this chapter, I give you a few tips on surviving the quest for bridal beauty with your sanity and bank account intact, as well as how to keep everyone else in the bridal party looking good.

Dress Shopping: What to Know

Until a few years ago, many wedding dresses were overdone and fussy creations that made every bride look like a glittery cream puff. Then Vera Wang and some other designers came along and streamlined the wedding dress, creating a variety of silhouettes and shapes to flatter every bride and body type. With so many options available today, it's nice to have an idea of what dresses appeal to you before you trudge out to the bridal salons.

Determining Your Wedding Gown Style

- ❍ What time of year will you be getting married? (Don't wear chiffon in winter or velvet in summer.)

- ❍ What parts of your body are your favorite, and what parts would you like to camouflage?

○ Where will your wedding take place? A church wedding might call for covered shoulders or a more modest neckline.

○ How formal is your wedding?

Don't buy your wedding dress before you can answer these questions. If you haven't settled on a time of year or venue, hold off on buying the dress, even if you fall in love with one. The gown you adore may end up being totally wrong for the wedding you eventually plan, and then you'll be stuck with an inappropriate dress or you'll have to break your budget buying a new one.

DO **Go Gown Surfing**

The Internet is a great place to look for wedding gowns. Hop on The Knot (www.theknot.com) and search through thousands of gowns by designer, style, or price. This is a fabulous way to look without accumulating more weighty (and pricey) wedding mags.

Okay, now it's okay to dig out those bridal magazines I told you to banish. They are chock-full of pictures of wedding gowns. As a matter of fact, most bridal magazines seem to be entirely made up of ads for wedding dresses. Flip through them and see which gowns appeal to you. Rip out your favorites, and compare them to see what the dresses have in common. Are you drawn to poofy ball gowns with elaborate embroidery or simple sheaths with no embellishment? Do you like certain necklines or maybe sheer sleeves? Knowing what styles you like will help the shopping process go smoother once you're in the salons.

Where to Go

Armed with your wedding gown research, where do you start shopping? Don't think you're limited to just the traditional bridal salons listed in your phone book. You have many options when it comes to finding your perfect dress.

The simplest and easiest route is a bridal salon. Most towns have one or two shops devoted exclusively to wedding dresses. Go to at least one salon to get the experience of being a pampered bride. You might also have a large discount superstore such as David's Bridal nearby. Don't expect to be treated with kid gloves here, but the extra work may be worth the bargains you find. If you don't have a discount store nearby but the thought of paying retail for your gown makes you shudder, consider looking in nontraditional places for your dress.

Finding Dresses off the Beaten Path

○ **Consignment stores.** Sometimes you can find vintage or barely used gowns.

○ **Seamstress.** If you can't find exactly what you want out there, find a great seamstress to make it for you.

○ **Internet.** You can buy gowns from online retailers or individuals (like on eBay). Just be careful about knowing the return policy.

○ **Evening gowns.** A bridesmaid's dress or off-the-rack evening gown in white or ivory may be perfect for a simpler wedding or bride.

Going Prepared

Regardless of the type of store you visit, you need to plan ahead to make the most of your expedition. My best advice is to not try to pack all your bridal-salon-hopping into one day. You may think you'll have enough energy to visit three shops in a row, but after a few hours of trying on gowns, they'll all blend together. Spread your visits out over a few weeks. And if at all possible, try to go on a weekday. Saturdays and Sundays are mayhem for bridal salons. Even a weekday evening will be quieter and you'll get more personal attention.

My second-best piece of advice when it comes to shopping for wedding dresses is not to bring an audience. We all know it can be more fun to shop with a friend, but bringing along all your bridesmaids and your mother is asking for trouble. Bring one friend (or your mother) to give you honest feedback, but choose carefully. This is not the time to bring your most cynical pal or a competitive girlfriend who'll end up trying on dresses next to you—and look better in them!

What to Bring to the Bridal Salon

○ Pictures of gowns you like from magazines and the Internet.

○ Nice underwear and a strapless bra (or you'll get stuck borrowing an old ratty one from the salon).

○ Shoes of the approximate heel height you want to wear for your wedding.

○ A notebook so you can take notes as you go along. After you leave the store, it can be hard to remember.

○ Bottled water and light snacks. This is hard work, and it is easy to get tired and cranky.

No matter how much you love the first dress you try on, don't be in a rush to plunk down your credit card and call it a day. Take your time to shop around and try on many styles of wedding gowns. You never know which gown may look great on you, even if it doesn't look like much on the hanger.

Most important, listen to your heart when you select your gown. You should have a very special feeling when you slip it on. After all, it's really all about the babe in the white dress!

Unfortunately, how happy your wedding dress shopping experience is will depend greatly on the saleswoman assigned to you. I have had brides have wildly different experiences at the same salon because the personalities of the saleswomen were so different. Don't be afraid to ask for someone new if you aren't happy with who has been assigned to you. Speak to a manager and make a new appointment, if necessary.

Sad Story/Happy Ending

One of my fun-loving, impulsive brides fell in love with a dress when she was visiting a friend in New York. Knowing she wouldn't be back for a while, she decided to buy the dress even though she hadn't been to any other salons. Sure enough, months later she could barely remember the dress and had major regrets because she hadn't tried on enough dresses to really be able to compare and contrast. She could barely sleep for weeks before the dress arrived because she was so nervous that she'd made the wrong decision and would be stuck with a dress she didn't love anymore. She'd spent so much on the first dress there was no way she could afford to buy a new dress if it didn't work. Luckily, when she tried on the dress again it was perfect for her. But she could have saved herself lots of heartache and worry by shopping around first.

Order Up!

After you've tried on so many gowns you don't ever want to see white again and have found the perfect dress, it's time to order. No matter what type of shop you work with, there are some business basics to know about the wedding dress world.

What to Look for in Your Wedding Dress Order

○ The agreed-upon price for the dress and any additional fees (estimate of alterations, shipping, plus size, etc.).

○ Your wedding date and estimated delivery date.

○ The cancellation and deposit policy.

○ Details of the gown, including color, your accurate measurements, style, and manufacturer.

It's crucial to get everything in writing when you're ordering your dress. Pay attention to what the salesclerk is writing down, and read the order carefully before you leave the store. Be careful of measurements, as well. Some stores have been known to inflate sizes so brides end up spending more for alterations later. On the other hand, don't insist on ordering a dress two sizes too small because you just know you're going to lose weight before the wedding. It is very difficult to let out a custom-made dress.

DON'T Take Their Word for It

You may have the nicest saleswoman in the world and trust every word she says, but if you don't have the details you discussed in writing on your order, you could be out of luck if she leaves the store. Or she may just forget that she quoted you a certain amount to add more beading on the train. Don't be stuck in a "she said, she said" argument months later. Get it all in writing.

Bridesmaids' Dresses: Would You Want to Wear This Again?

After you've completed the exhausting task of picking your dress, it's on to an even more tiring task: the bridesmaids' dresses. I have to admit that I think this can be one of the most tedious and frustrating parts of the entire planning process for brides. Who in their right mind thought it was a good idea to take a handful of women with different body types and personalities and put them in the same dress? Many alternatives have popped up in recent years to make this impossible task a bit more bearable, though.

Alternatives to Matching Bridesmaids' Dresses

○ Ask each woman to select a dress in a certain color. Black is the most popular, but I did a gorgeous summer wedding where each bridal attendant wore a different pink knee-length dress. Even though they didn't match, the overall look was lovely.

○ Select a company that will make different styles of dress in the same fabric and color. This way the color is identical, but each woman can select the most flattering look for her. Try www.simpledress.com.

○ For more casual weddings, ask your attendants to wear a dress of a certain length and let them pick the color and style.

A Matching Set

Even if you're hell bent on finding one dress for everyone, keep in mind that your friends will be paying for this. Either find something really inexpensive they won't care about tossing in the back of their closet, or make a huge effort to select something you would actually wear to a cocktail party. Some good bets for nonbridesmaids' dresses you actually would wear in public again are the off-the-rack retailers such as Anne Taylor, Talbots, BCBG Maz Azria, and Nicole Miller. Even J. Crew and Banana Republic are good options for casual, summery weddings.

Keep in mind that if you choose an odd color such as melon or chartreuse (even if it is hot right now), very few of your friends will look good in it, and it will be dated before the rice is thrown at the end of the night.

Remember this for your own photos, as well. Trendy colors don't stand the test of time and will date your wedding. I can pinpoint some of my past weddings to the year just by looking at the color of the bridesmaids' dresses.

The Business of Bridesmaids' Dresses

The best strategy for finalizing the bridesmaid's dress is to narrow the field down to a handful you like and then ask for your friends' opinions. You can take a vote or just take their feedback into consideration. It isn't a bad idea to find a place where one of your bridesmaids can try on the gown. We all know that a dress can look entirely different in person than in the pages of a magazine. Colors are usually off in ads as well. Get swatches of the fabric you choose to share with florists, because what is teal to one person is sea foam green to another.

DO Be Clear on Finances

Be up front with your bridesmaids about what they will be responsible for paying for. If they are paying for their own dresses, have them pay the salon individually (if possible) so you won't have to act as the bank. There's nothing more uncomfortable than chasing down a bridesmaid for a check.

Once you've settled on a dress, you need to get all your bridesmaids' measurements. Either arrange for them to come into the shop where you've selected the dress or have them get measured by a tailor in their own town and send you the numbers. It isn't a good idea for bridesmaids to measure themselves. It is difficult to do properly, and it is too tempting to shave a few inches off with intentions of losing weight. Place the order for all the dresses at once to ensure that the fabric is cut from the same dye lot and that they arrive together.

If you insist on matching shoes or jewelry, this might be a nice thing for you to pay for. If you are a little more flexible, ask your bridesmaids to select their own shoes in a complementing color. I had one wedding where the bridesmaids each picked different silver sandals to go with a pale blue dress and it looked great. Don't obsess over matching pantyhose, seamless underwear, or other things that will make your bridesmaids grumble about you for years to come.

If you want your girls to wear nude hose, let them know, but don't give them the brand and style. They might choke you with them later.

Powder Blue Tuxedos and Other Crimes of Fashion

When it comes to dressing the guys, it's more important to choose a style that fits the wedding than conforms to strict etiquette rules. Even though Emily Post might spin in her grave, I have many weddings where the groomsmen wear black tuxedos before the perfectly proper hour of 6 o'clock. I don't, however, recommend white tie and tails for a morning wedding. It just doesn't fit.

Determine the formality of your wedding, what the weather will be like, and the time of day before choosing the men's attire. For many weddings, a classic black tuxedo is the perfect answer. If your wedding is a bit different, you might consider some alternatives.

Options Beyond the Penguin Suit

- **White dinner jacket.** This is great for warm-weather weddings.
- **Dark suit.** A beautiful designer suit can even outshine a tux.
- **Blazer and pants.** For a casual or outdoor wedding, khaki pants and a navy blazer can look great.
- **Pants and a linen shirt.** This is the perfect option for a beach or tropical wedding.

Whatever style you choose, it is important to be sure everyone is on the same page. It is okay to have all your groomsmen wear their own black tuxedos as long as the styles are similar. Don't have one guy in a double-breasted style, one in a shawl collar, and one wearing an ascot. Your groomsmen should wear the same style tie and vest/cummerbund, which can be great things to give them as a gift. Consider substituting straight black ties for the more old-fashioned bow tie as a way to update a classic tux.

Looking Your Best Without Looking Like a Drag Queen

We've all seen the bride who had her hair teased so high it's a wonder she could fit through the doors of the church. What happens to normal women that compels them to slap on so much makeup that even their fiancé has a hard time recognizing them? I can only chalk it up to bridal dementia: the illness that takes over previously normal women and convinces them they must look like a completely different person on their wedding day.

Looking Like Yourself, Only Better

The best bridal hair and makeup help the bride look stunning without making her look so dramatically different that no one in her family recognizes her. It is important to try out your stylists ahead of time so you can be sure they understand the look you're going for. Keep in mind that wedding day hair and makeup usually needs to be a bit heavier so it will last the many hours it needs to and stand up under the flash of cameras. Nevertheless, you shouldn't feel like you're suffocating under the weight of it.

Wedding Beauty Tips

○ Do all your facials and waxings at least 2 weeks before your wedding in case you react badly to the treatments.

○ Do your final haircut and color 2 weeks before the wedding, as well. Don't try any new color or cut right before the wedding.

○ Don't try any new makeup on the wedding day. Even if you're using a makeup artist, bring your own foundation to avoid allergic reactions.

○ Pack a small bag with pressed powder and the lipstick color you plan to wear on the wedding day. If you can swing it, have your hairstylist and makeup artist stay and retouch you after the ceremony.

○ Don't forget that special perfume—but don't overdo it, either.

Finding the Perfect Stylist

Not to sound like a broken record, but the best way to find great wedding hair specialists and makeup artists is by word of mouth. Ask other wedding vendors (especially photographers) and brides who they recommend. You'll invariably hear the same names popping up over and over.

You can either opt to have the stylists come to your home or hotel room, or go to a salon on your wedding day. Both have pros and cons. Having stylists come to you is certainly the most convenient way to go. It does cost more for this luxury, and not all brides want to turn their hotel room into a salon. On the other hand, some brides just can't deal with the hustle and bustle of a beauty salon before their wedding, even if it is less costly.

DON'T Skip the Trial

Be sure to do a trial with both your hairstylist and makeup artist before the wedding. Allow plenty of time to grow out your hair if you need to, and take your headpiece so you can practice the finished look. Even if the trial is an extra expense, it's worth every penny.

You don't have to hire professionals to do your hair and makeup if you are extremely confident in your own skills or have talented bridesmaids. Be sure to practice before the big day, though, and keep it simple. If you plan to do your own makeup, check out www.bridalbabe.com for great wedding makeup tips and even do-it-yourself kits. Even better, invest in a makeup lesson from a professional or make an appointment at your favorite makeup counter for a wedding makeover.

Making Up the Maids and Moms

One of the questions I get every week (or so it seems) is whether or not a bride should treat her bridesmaids and mother to salon services. There is no hard-and-fast answer to this. It depends on your budget (did you allow for this expense back in Chapter 3?) and your preference.

If you must have every girl wearing identical updos, it's only fair that you pay for it. It is a lovely gesture to offer hair and makeup to your bridesmaids even if you don't dictate a certain look. This can be your gift to them, as well. Keep in mind that not everyone is comfortable getting these things done by an unfamiliar stylist, so you can always offer one or both as options and let your girls choose for themselves. It is a fun thing to do together, whether at a salon or in the hotel.

When it comes to moms, you should offer the services to both if you offer them to either. It starts things off on a sour note if your mother is treated to hair and makeup with the bridesmaids and the groom's mother is left out in the cold. Treating them to a little pampering is a lovely way to show appreciation for the mothers and to include them in the getting-ready fun.

Looking the Part

Do	Don't
✓ Be prepared when you shop for bridal gowns.	✗ Forget to read the dress order carefully.
✓ Be considerate of budget and body type when selecting bridesmaids' dresses.	✗ Keep track of bridesmaids' dress payments.
✓ Select men's formalwear based on your wedding's style.	✗ Be afraid to skip the black tuxedo.
✓ Test your wedding hair and makeup before the big day.	✗ Try any new beauty treatments 2 weeks before the wedding.

11

A Rose by Any Other Name ...

When it's time to think about the décor for your wedding, you might think all you need to do is choose some colors and find a willing florist. What could be simpler, right? Well, maybe and maybe not. Modern wedding décor encompasses much more than bouquets and centerpieces, so it pays to know your options before you go talk to a florist. In this chapter, I tell you what to remember when working with a florist and what not to get suckered into. I also tell you how to personalize your wedding without going overboard.

Picking Flowers

Before you hurry out to your neighborhood florist ready to check another task off your wedding to-do list, you need to be prepared to really talk about all the décor for your wedding. You need to have a good number of decisions made already. As excited as you may be to talk about the bridal bouquet you've envisioned for the last 5 years, don't waste your time or a florist's time by being unprepared. I've had brides who insist on meeting with floral designers before they're ready, and we always have to drag ourselves back again because the first meetings were pretty pointless. This doesn't make for happy designers.

What to Know Before Meeting with Florists

○ **The dresses.** You should have selected your dress and the bridesmaid's dress (and preferably have a photo and fabric swatch of both). The dresses influence the personal flowers a great deal.

○ **Sites.** You should have all your sites locked in. Know which rooms you'll be using for each part of your wedding, from the ceremony to cocktail hour to dinner.

○ **Attendants.** Know how many bridal attendants you'll have on each side. It's great if you know how many ushers, readers, and grandparents will be attending as well.

○ **Reception info.** Know your guest count and the style of reception you'll have. Whether you do a standing cocktail party or a seated dinner makes a big difference to a floral decorator.

○ **Flowers you love and hate.** Flip through magazines and books, and pull out or copy photos of arrangements and flowers that appeal to you.

○ **Any flower allergies.** No one wants a groom sneezing through the ceremony because he's having a reaction to his boutonniere.

Even though selecting your flowers can be one of the most fun elements of wedding planning, it can also be overwhelming. Don't worry if you seem to like bright bouquets as well as soft pastels or if you're drawn to sleek modern designs some days but lush English garden styles the next. A good floral designer can help you define your style and even create a blend of two elements you love.

Sad Story/Happy Ending

One of my brides had a bridesmaid who was very allergic to flowers, so much so that the bride was worried that carrying a bouquet would make her friend's eyes swell up to the point she wouldn't be able to see to walk down the aisle! Although I never recommend silk flowers, I did suggest doing a silk floral bouquet for the allergic bridesmaid in this case. The florist matched the silk rose and real roses perfectly, and it was nearly impossible to tell the difference unless you got up close. And best of all, we had a happy bridesmaid!

When a Florist Isn't Just a Florist

You may notice I use the term *floral designer* more often than *florist*. The wedding industry has developed to such a point over the past several years that many wedding florists now incorporate other décor in their business. Whether it be lighting or props or fabric, these designers do much more than flowers. You may not need the services of a complete design team if you're just doing simple floral décor, but if you need a chuppah or an elaborate ceremony arch, these full-service designers may be your best bet.

DO Hire a Florist Who Specializes in Weddings

Even if your corner florist does lovely pick-me-up bouquets, she may not be the best choice for your wedding flowers. Florists who specialize in weddings usually provide more service on the wedding day and are used to dealing with wedding crises. You don't want a delivery guy dropping off your bouquets and then realize the flowers aren't what you envisioned. He won't be able to do much, but often a wedding florist will be able to fix things on the spot.

To find a good floral designer, ask your reception site for recommendations. They often know the best designers in town and which ones have worked well in their space before. It's great if your florist is familiar with your sites. He'll know what works in the space and what absolutely won't fly. Try to visit florist's websites so you can get a sense of each designer's style before you set up meetings. No sense in meeting with a super-modern floral designer when you have your heart set on a French country wedding.

The Perfect Proposal

When you meet with floral designers (armed with your swatches and magazine photos), be sure to ask to see a portfolio of their work. Communicate your ideas and then listen to theirs. Be up front about your budget, and give a firm number, if possible. After your meeting, you'll receive a proposal that outlines what you discussed.

DON'T Neglect to Read the Floral Proposal

I can't tell you the number of brides I've had over the years who don't bother to carefully read their floral proposal. One bride was shocked when a dome-shaped bouquet showed up on her wedding day despite the fact that it clearly read "dome-shaped bouquet" on her proposal. Read your proposal, and ask about any terms you don't understand.

After you've received proposals and settled on a floral designer, ask to do a walk-through of the spaces together. If you didn't have your initial meeting at your wedding site, this will be a great time to determine where everything will go and be sure you didn't miss any spots that need décor. Also, ask to see a sample centerpiece prior to your wedding day while you still have time to make any tweaks to the design.

Keep in mind that if you see a sample several months before your wedding, you might not see the exact flowers you'll get on your wedding day due to seasonality of blooms.

DO **Plan Ahead**

If you want your guests to take home the flowers at the end of the night, ask your florist if the flowers can be designed to lift out of the containers or if the containers can be taken at the end of the night, too. If you'd like to have the flowers delivered to your home or donated to a hospital, make arrangements with your florist ahead of time for the redelivery.

Remember that flowers are affected by things such as weather and shipping. I've known a late frost and a UPS strike to cause flowers to arrive damaged or not at all. Keep in mind that sometimes your floral designer can't do anything about this and may make substitutions. If this concerns you, ask up front what flowers he would substitute. But also be prepared to roll with the punches when it comes to Mother Nature.

Simple Elegance or Simply Excessive?

Décor is such a fun part of wedding planning that it can easily get out of hand. After all, the way your wedding looks is a big part of expressing your personal style on your wedding day. But keep in mind that you don't have to blow half your budget on flowers to create a beautiful and unique look.

What Do You Mean "It's Not in Season"?

One of the biggest road blocks my brides stumble over on the path to floral perfection is falling in love with flowers they just can't have or can't have unless they're willing to pay a fortune. Although the availability of flowers is improving dramatically with blooms coming in from Holland and South America at all times of the year, some varieties are still pricey or unavailable unless you hit the season just right. After a lovely nosegay of lily of the valley appeared on a magazine cover, I had droves of brides insisting they had to carry this down the aisle—until they heard the price for the tiny, out-of-season lily of the valley bouquet.

If you want to keep your floral budget under control, ask what flowers are in season on your wedding day. It's much better to know your options up front than to fall in love with a look based on something well out of your price range. Often, your floral designer can recommend a flower with a similar look to the one you have your heart set on. Or if you must indulge in a pricey flower, use it sparingly. Perhaps embellish a rose bouquet with touches of lily of the valley instead of blowing your budget on an all lily of the valley bouquet.

What Not to Skimp on and What to Lose

When you meet with floral designers, you'll be asked about more types of décor than you ever thought possible. You may never have thought about whether you want pew flowers or wreaths on the door of the church or an arrangement in the ladies' room until you're confronted with a million options. Keep in mind that it's the designer's job to offer you all the options. Also keep in mind that you don't have to do all of them. Certain things will make a big impact, and others are just more window dressing.

Floral Décor Not to Skimp On

○ **Centerpieces.** A mirror tile and a votive candle do not a centerpiece make. Your tables will look bare if you leave the space in the middle virtually open.

A Rose by Any Other Name ...

○ **Corsages and boutonnieres for family members.** Don't try to save money by skipping the grandmothers. It's amazing how honored family members are when they are remembered with flowers. Don't cut corners and hurt feelings.

○ **Escort card or entrance table arrangement.** This is the first thing guests see when they enter your reception, and first impressions are everything. It doesn't have to be over the top, but this is the place where guests will stop to sign the guest book or pick up their seating assignment, so make it worth the stop.

As with all the other elements of wedding planning, focus your budget on the most noticeable parts, and guests will come away with the impression that your wedding was much more expensive than it actually was. If the most prominent décor is well done, people won't miss all the little extras. Now, if you have cash to blow on décor, by all means load up on door wreaths, garlands, and pew arrangements. But if you don't, you can lose some extras without losing style.

Décor You Can Afford to Lose

○ Ceremony décor beyond two nice altar arrangements. Door wreaths, pew flowers, greenery swags on railings, and additional altar arrangements are all extras.

○ Cocktail table flowers. Your guests only pause here for an hour at the most and not all will even make it to a table, so just put some votive candles out and scatter some flower petals if you want to save a bit.

○ Décor on the cake table. Don't splurge for garlands and lots of extra flowers here. Arrange the bridesmaids' bouquets around the cake for a lovely effect (especially if you have a lot of attendants).

○ Arrangements in the ladies' rooms and on the bars. These are active areas, so don't clutter them with flowers.

DO Reuse Flowers

Don't let flowers go to waste. If you can take the altar arrangements from your ceremony, ask your florist to transport them to your reception to be used on buffet tables or on either side of the band. Put bridesmaids' bouquets around the cake, on cocktail tables, or on mantles. Place your bridal bouquet in an empty vase, and use it as the centerpiece on your sweetheart table. Tie pew flowers to the backs of the chairs at the head table. Just be sure to arrange for your florist to take care of the switch.

Nonfloral Décor: Beyond Bouquets and Bubble Bowls

Sometimes some of the biggest impact in wedding décor comes from things that have nothing to do with flowers. You can completely transform a room with the proper lighting or dress up ugly ballroom chairs with pretty chair covers. Sometimes it's easier to give your wedding site a facelift through lighting and rentals than trying to douse it in flowers.

Bring It in and Jazz It Up

Most areas have at least one rental company that provides everything from tables and chairs to linens and china. If you're lucky enough to be in a larger city, you might have several options for specialty rentals right in your backyard. Even if you don't live near some of these fabulous rental companies, many now ship all over the country so you can still get the upscale options whisked right to your door.

A Rose by Any Other Name ...

Don't underestimate the impact changing a chair or table linen can have on your wedding look. A fabulous tablecloth can instantly add color and depth to a room and make your flowers even more dramatic, and often at a reasonable price. Often if you have a great linen to add impact, you can go simpler on floral décor.

Ways to Use Rentals as Décor

- ❍ Bring in chair covers to mask hideous banquet chairs. This can dress up a room instantly.

- ❍ Select special linens for the escort card table, sweetheart table, and cake table. This will add some punch without adding lots to your bottom line.

- ❍ Bring in ornate votive candles or beaded lamps for your cocktail tables, and skip floral décor.

- ❍ Rent a beautiful base plate for a big impact when guests are seated for dinner and then use the standard china for the rest of the meal. Guests will remember the first impression.

- ❍ Use a colored water goblet with the standard wine glasses for a beautiful look without a big cost.

When bringing in rental equipment, always appoint someone to inventory it and collect it at the end of the night. Arrange for the rental company to deliver and pick up on the same day, if possible, to avoid things sitting around and getting misplaced. You do have to pay for missing items!

Light It Up

Lighting is one of the most overlooked aspects of wedding décor, but it can be one of the most important. If you don't have proper lighting, no one will be able to see the stunning centerpieces you spent so much money on. You can actually spend less on flowers if you spend a little on lighting to show them off. Whether you use a professional lighting design company or rely on heavy use of candles, incorporate lighting into your décor budget and overall plan.

DO Take a Lighting Walk-Through

Check out both your ceremony and reception sites at the time of day (and year) your wedding will be held. Notice how the light affects the room. If it is bright as day outside, maybe that candlelight ceremony won't work as well as you planned. Find out when sunset will be on your wedding day, and be sure to plan around it. You don't want to be having cocktails outside in the dark because you didn't think ahead to consider the time.

Common Lighting Options

○ **Candles.** The least-expensive lighting option can also be the most romantic. Use a variety of heights to get the maximum glow throughout the room.

○ **Pinspotting.** You can also use beams of light focused on floral centerpieces from above. This is a wonderful way to increase impact in a room because it makes flowers pop in a dimmed room.

○ **Color washes.** Large colored lights can be used on tent ceilings and dance floors.

○ **Gobos.** Patterned light can be customized, such as a bride and groom's monogram, and projected onto dance floors, walls, or ceilings.

Sometimes a floral designer will be able to provide some lighting options, but if not, check with your site. Some hotels have in-house lighting staff, which can be a great value. Or they can recommend an independent lighting designer who can do everything from landscape lighting to custom gobos.

Dressing Up a Tent

If you're planning a reception in a tent, budget in a little money to transform the tent from utilitarian to magical. It pays to think ahead when bringing in a tent so you can anticipate any visual challenges. Don't wait until your wedding day to be surprised by orange water barrels holding down your tent.

The quickest way to dress up a tent is with fabric. Fabric tent liners instantly hide the beams and inner structure of a frame tent so it looks much softer. There's nothing more sterile than seeing lots of metal tent beams and supports. If you select a pole tent that has no metal beams, you should still plan on covering the center and side poles with some fabric. If a tent must be weighted with water barrels, arrange for these to be covered with white tablecloths. Water barrels usually aren't too pretty.

Lighting is important when you're working with a tent because often the tent has no source of light except what you bring in. Color washes or string lights behind fabric liners can provide a soft ambient light. Edging the perimeter of the tent with string lights is another popular option.

Another great way to soften tents is with plants. Cluster palm trees around center tent poles, and bunch potted ferns around side poles and tent stakes. This also serves as a great way to bring attention to the stakes so people don't trip on them. You can usually rent plants through a plant rental company or your floral designer so you won't be stuck with dozens of ferns after your wedding.

Décor

Do	Don't
✓ Be ready when you meet florists.	✗ Insist on out-of-season flowers.
✓ Hire a floral designer who specializes in weddings.	✗ Overlook rentals as a way to dress up a room.
✓ Soften a tent with fabric and lighting.	✗ Forget that lighting can help maximize your flowers.

12

Lights, Camera, Action!

So you've set the wedding date, booked a site, and even hired a caterer. Time to kick back and relax for a while, right? Wrong!

Photography and videography are elements of your wedding your guests won't notice (unless you hire an absolute disaster who hits on all your bridesmaids) but will provide your only lasting records of the day. In this chapter, I tell you how to select a good photographer and videographer, what tricks to avoid, how to save money and get exactly what you want, and how to ensure that your wedding day is captured just the way you'd like it to be.

Don't Say Cheese: Finding the Right Match

We've all been to weddings where the photographer or videographer was a walking disaster. Either he was intrusive and spent so much time posing the bride and groom they missed most of their wedding, or he changed film during the ceremony so loudly no one could hear the vows. I'm here to tell you it doesn't have to be this way, and not all wedding photographers are cheese-balls. For the most part, wedding photographers and videographers are professional and unobtrusive, but it's always the one or two bad eggs that make the rest look bad.

With photography and videography, I've found that you always get what you pay for. Once in a blue moon you can find a rising star who charges much less than he's worth, but don't spend too much time looking for this mythical creature. I've only discovered a handful in all the years I've planned weddings, and they didn't stay underpriced for very long.

Personality Is King

With that said, there are some important things to look for when you're shopping around for a photographer or videographer. The most important thing is personality. I think this can be even more important than how much you like his or her work. Remember that you will be spending a lot of time with this person on your wedding day. If you find them annoying or abrasive, it will only get worse after a few hours together, and your pictures and video will likely show your irritation.

Say It with Style

After personality, pay attention to quality of work. Look through sample albums of entire weddings, not just a portfolio of the best shots. Lots of photographers can get a few great shots out of a wedding, but you want to see how consistent their work is throughout the entire event.

DON'T Fall for These Photography Tricks

When interviewing photographers and videographers, be sure to see the work of the actual shooter who will be at your wedding. If you're hiring one of the studio's junior shooters, insist on seeing his or her photography. There might be quite a difference from what the studio shows on its website. Don't fall for the old "bait and switch" trick where you assume you're hiring a well-known shooter but the studio sends someone else instead. Always request that the name of the shooter be put in your contract. Some big-name photographers will show up to shoot the portraits and then leave someone else to shoot the rest of your wedding. This might be fine with you, but ask about it up front.

Look at the style of shooting. Do they do lots of posed shots or mostly photojournalism? Be sure your style fits the photographer's style. Photojournalism is a photography style that is more documentary in nature, so don't fall in love with a photojournalist who doesn't do any posed photos and then hand him a list of 50 family group shots on the wedding day. You won't be happy with the portraits, and the photographer definitely won't be happy with you.

Find out how each photographer presents the work. Does he do traditional bound leather albums or more offbeat coffee table albums? If you have your heart set on your best friend's collage-style album, be sure your photographer can do it for you. I'm not, however, advocating choosing a mediocre photographer just because he can do the miniature albums you think would be perfect for your parents. Remember, it doesn't matter how cute the album is if the photos aren't great!

The Digital Debate

Next you'll want to check if he shoots digital or film. Both are fabulous mediums, so you can't go wrong either way, but it is good to know the advantages to both.

Digital photography has revolutionized the industry by eliminating the expense of film and processing, providing instant gratification for shooters and making retouching a snap. Digital photographers no longer keep track of how much they shoot because they don't have to worry about the cost of film. This means my brides now can have upward of a thousand photos to choose from. Of course, then your problem is how to narrow those down to a 50-picture album!

This isn't to say film isn't still a wonderful option. Many strict photojournalists prefer to shoot in film for the look it gives them. If you love the idea of negatives and proofs, film might be the best option for you. Don't expect to dictate film or digital to a photographer, though. If you are dead-set on one or the other, be sure you find out what a photographer shoots before you go meet with him.

Questions to Ask Your Photographer

○ Do you shoot digital or film or a combination of both?

○ If you shoot film, is there a limit on the number rolls of film you shoot? (Try to get unlimited film, if possible.)

○ Can I specify the amount of color versus black and white? Can I request sepia and infrared photos?

○ Will I get paper proofs, a magazine proof book, or online proofs?

○ What will you wear to the wedding? (If the wedding is black tie, let your photographer know.)

○ How many assistants will you bring? How many are shooters? (Don't assume every assistant can shoot. Some are just for holding lights and carrying bags, so specify if you want a second shooter.)

○ Do you have back-up cameras?

○ Do you set up lights? (Light stands should be kept to a minimum to avoid intrusion. Ask if they're stationary or if they'll roll around. Stationary lights are less intrusive. Sometimes additional lighting is needed in dark rooms, though, so ask if they can bounce the light or use umbrellas to soften it.)

○ Can I get my negatives or high-resolution files? (Be aware there's a difference between low-resolution files and high-resolution files, and ask for the high if you plan on printing decent pictures from them.)

○ Do you have liability insurance? (All reputable photographers will.)

○ How do you work with videographers? (Be sure your photographer is willing to play nice with others. You don't want a vendor war on your wedding day.)

Getting a Deal ... or Not

It's true that wedding photography and videography are not cheap. *Good* photography and videography, I should say. Plenty of bargain-basement photographers are out there shooting, and even more amateurs buy a camera and consider themselves professionals. Be very wary of a deal that seems too good to be true.

Focus on Budget

Depending on your priorities, wedding photography may take up a nice chunk of your overall budget, or it may be something you'd rather not go overboard on. Depending on your area, you could spend anywhere from several hundred dollars to several thousand dollars in each area. If you're a film buff, you might decide to hire a top videographer who shoots with movie film and a lower-priced photographer. Or you may divide up your budget evenly between the two. Try to prioritize photography and videography, and shop first for the one that's most important to you.

Don't Shoot Yourself in the Foot

Even if you decide to cut back in this area so you can have the band of your dreams, don't make a mistake that will have long-lasting effects. Remember that after the guests go home and the caterer packs it in, your photos and video are all you have left to remember your big day.

Photography and Videography Money-Saving Mistakes to Avoid

○ Don't expect a relative or family friend to be a good option unless they are an experienced professional. It's too easy for them to get distracted by playing dual roles as a guest and worker bee.

○ If you ask your uncle to videotape the wedding, don't expect the quality to be any better than a shaky home movie. And don't get upset afterward if it isn't what you had hoped for. Saving some money here isn't worth damaging relationships or hurting feelings.

○ If you hire someone who is just starting out because they have great prices, be warned that you may pay for their inexperience in the end. I've heard of new photographers who forget to load film in their cameras or overexpose every shot.

○ Be aware that if you hire someone who turns over the film or tape to you at the end of the night, you will have to do all the leg work to get prints, albums, and finished videotapes made. Be sure the savings is worth the extra effort.

○ Don't expect the disposable cameras you put on guest tables to provide you with great reception shots. Most guests will forget to use the flash or take out-of-focus shots you can't even use. The cameras and the processing can add up to several hundred dollars that might be better spent on your professional photographer.

Instead of wasting money on disposable cameras or risking your wedding memories on an inexperienced photographer, hire a reputable photographer and videographer. You don't have to get all the bells and whistles or spring for the most expensive package, but spend your money on quality. You can save up and buy an expensive album later, but you can never recapture the moments of your wedding day.

Bye, Bye Packages

Photography and videography can be two of the most confusing areas of wedding planning because everyone does things a little bit differently. Nothing is apples to apples!

Lights, Camera, Action!

My best advice is to toss out the packages. That's right. Instead of going along with what someone else wants to sell you, take some time to figure out what you need. In a way, create your own package. This way you won't get stuck with a gigantic wall portrait you'll never hang or parents' albums when all your mom really wants are photos to frame and put in the living room.

What Do You Need?

Now, before my photographer and videographer friends start coming after me with torches and pitchforks, I should clarify: by no means do I mean for you to ignore the pricing you're given and try to make up your own price. I simply mean you should educate yourself on what is important to you. This way, when you get presented with choices of the Platinum, Gold, and Tinfoil packages, you will be able to determine which comes closest to your needs and how you can add or substitute to get all the elements you really want.

Considerations When Designing a Photography Package

- How many hours of coverage will you really need? Do you want them to shoot you getting ready or just start at the ceremony? Do you want them to stay until the bitter end or just until the last major event (like the cake cutting)?

- Is it important to you for the photographer or videographer to have an assistant or a second shooter?

- Do you want paper proofs? In an increasingly digital market, these are becoming less and less common and often cost extra.

- Do you want an album? Do your parents want albums?

- Do you want an engagement portrait or bridal portrait sitting?

- Will you want lots of reprints? If you plan on buying lots (say to use for a holiday card), you should negotiate this price up front.

133

○ Do you want online posting of your wedding photos?

○ Do you want to keep your negatives or high-resolution files?

○ How many copies of your video do you want? On DVD or VHS?

○ Do you want highlight reels, interviews, or photo montages on your video?

Negotiating with Confidence

When you've answered these questions and have a good sense of what you'd like (in an ideal world, of course), you can approach photographers and videographers with more confidence and negotiating skills.

Many photographers and videographers will be happy to give you a price for all the elements you have prioritized and make a custom package that fits your needs. This doesn't mean every photographer or videographer will be falling all over themselves to customize something for you or that you can always get everything your little heart desires. For example, some photographers and videographers don't give up negatives or unedited footage. If this is their firm policy, don't try to talk them out of it. If it's a deal-breaker for you, just find someone who doesn't mind parting with them.

Locking It In

When you've found a good match for your style and budget, get a contract and put down a deposit. Good photographers and videographers book up quickly and can usually only do one wedding a day. Don't expect them to hold a date for you, either. Even if they promise to give you the right of first refusal on the date, don't kick back and assume you can just wait until they call you. Remember that even though this may be the most important day of your life, it is still business for the vendors you hire.

DO **Read the Fine Print**

Be sure to read your contract carefully. This may sound like a no-brainer, but you'd be surprised at the number of brides who sign a contract and then get upset when they later realize they won't be curling up to watch their wedding video as soon as they get back from their honeymoon. Many of the top videographers take a little longer to edit, so be sure to pay attention to the time frame they give you for the completed video. Also, be sure to give any photos, music selections, or invitations to them if they request them. They can't produce the final video without them, and you'll just be holding up the process.

Your contract might be a simple letter of agreement or a multi-page legal document that spells out every contingency plan. Either way, it is important to remember to spell everything out. If the photographer makes a promise to do something or include something extra, be sure it's in the contract. Getting it in writing helps everyone remember what was agreed upon. Good communication with all your wedding vendors is crucial for worry-free wedding planning.

The Dreaded List

If you want to ensure that your photographer will hate you, hand him a four-page list of every possible combination of family and guests known to man and then tell him you want lots of photos. Brides often don't realize they're tying their photographer's hands when they come up with a list of "must-have" shots longer than their actual guest list.

The photo lists you find in most bridal magazines are usually so rudimentary they make photographers want to rip out their hair. Don't bother giving this list to your photographer; it will be virtually useless to him unless this is his first wedding, in which case, best of luck. You should, however, make a short list of the important group shots you really must have. Keep this list to half a page at the very most.

How to Compile Your Must-Have Photo List

○ Break the list down into photos that can be taken before the wedding, ones that should be taken after the ceremony, and groups that can wait until later in the reception (like sorority sisters or friends from high school).

○ List the names so your photographer can call them out easily. Writing down "Jones family" is too general and will result in Aunt Ethel getting left out and you having to hear about it for the rest of your life.

○ Assign a family member from each side to help the photographer gather the groups. Your photographer won't know what your cousins look like, but your sister will.

○ Make a short list of some of the most important elements of your wedding. Don't assume your photographer will know that you spent weeks making the menu cards and want close-up photos of them unless you tell him.

Sad Story/Happy Ending

One of my brides wore the veil her grandmother had worn on her wedding day, but she neglected to mention how important it was to me or to the photographer. When she got her photos back, she was heartbroken to see there were almost no full-length shots of the veil. Of course, this heirloom veil was news to me! Luckily, the photographer agreed to re-shoot portraits of her in her gown, and we were able to add them to her wedding photos.

Filming Your Wedding Day

If the thought of huge video cameras at your ceremony and the prospect of your guests having microphones shoved in their faces sends chills down your spine, forget your worries. Wedding videography has advanced leaps and bounds over the past several years. Today's best videographers are more like moviemakers than anything else. A great videographer will capture the mood and emotion of the day and get some of those unforgettable moments.

Choose with Care

As in the photography industry, though, there are plenty of fly-by-night video operations that are a far cry from the professionals. Be very careful when selecting a videographer, because a bad one can be intrusive and make your guests cringe.

Checklist of Videographer Warning Signs

- If prices are dirt cheap, there's a reason.

- An abrasive personality or sloppy appearance. Enough said.

- If you only see demo samples and never a full wedding, be warned. Anyone can edit dozens of weddings into a decent demo, but seeing a whole edited wedding will give you a better idea of what your video will be like. Look at a few videos so you can see if the work is consistent.

- Listen for good sound during the ceremony. Can you hear the vows, or are they very faint? Do they use actual music from the reception or dub in CDs afterward?

- A "my way or the highway" approach. If the videographer insists on interviewing guests when you don't want this or tells you he must have bright lights at your reception, keep looking.

Shopping the Shooters

When you've found a videographer who has a good reputation, does beautiful work, and is easy to get along with, it's time to get down to the nitty-gritty. Ask for references, and look at lots of samples of their work, preferably at the location where you'll be getting married (or similar locations). Ask your wedding planner and other vendors if they're familiar with the videographer's reputation. Often the wedding industry knows more about reputations than your friends will.

DO **Share the Rules**

Be sure to find out from your ceremony site and officiant if there are any rules regarding photography and videography during the ceremony. Tell your photographer and videographer before the wedding day so they can plan accordingly.

Questions to Ask Your Videographer

○ How many cameras will they use? The more angles, the better the coverage. (For best results, you should have at least two.) Is the second camera manned or stationary?

○ How new is your equipment, and do you have backup? (Cameras get outdated quickly. The newest professional cameras are smaller and use less light than the old bulky dinosaurs, which means they are less obtrusive.)

○ What do you wear to the wedding? (If you want your shooters in black tie, specify it.)

○ What type of microphones do you use? (It's best if lavalieres are used on the groom, officiant, podium where readings will take place, and near the music during the ceremony. If they can't do this, where would they hide mics so they could pick up audio?)

Lights, Camera, Action!

○ What type of lights do you use? (Lights during ceremonies are intrusive, especially in churches, and should be avoided. Any lights during receptions should be as soft as possible.)

○ How long will the finished video be? (Specify if you want a short version or the unedited footage. Specify if you want DVDs or VHS tapes. Most people want DVDs today because the quality is much higher and they last longer.)

○ How long after the wedding will it take to finish my video? (Quality editing takes time, so be prepared to be patient. Let them know ahead of time if you want highlight tapes or photo montages.)

○ Do you edit your own work, or does another person edit the video?

○ Do you have liability insurance? (If the answer is no, run away!)

○ How do you work with photographers? (It's important that your vendors get along and don't spend your wedding day fighting for shots.)

○ If you haven't worked at my site before, will you visit it prior to the wedding or attend the rehearsal?

DO Highlight Your Day

Only your blood relatives will want to sit through the hours of your full-length wedding video, and even they may not be up to it. Suck it up and get a highlight tape, which is a shorter version of your wedding day usually set to music. This 5- to 20-minute tape will capture the highlights of the day and is perfect to pop in when friends come over. Or have your videographer edit the tape tightly, shortening up the prayers, homily, toasts, etc. Save the long version for your own entertainment and posterity.

Speak Up!

Communicating your wishes is the best way to get the photos and video you want. This doesn't mean you should spend your wedding day acting as director. That's another way to get on the fast train to Bridezilla land. Instead, you should be clear about your expectations before the wedding. If you expect your photographer to take shots of the guests at each table, tell him. If you want to be sure your videographer doesn't interview the guests, spell it out.

It's crucial to communicate the schedule of the wedding day and any last-minute changes to both your photographer and videographer. If you're planning to have all your guests ring bells as you leave the church, be sure to let your photographer and videographer know, or they might miss the moment.

Photography and Videography

Do	Don't
✓ Find a photographer and videographer whose personality fits with yours.	✗ Assume you must select a preset package of services.
✓ Read the contract carefully.	✗ Neglect to include the name of your shooter in the contract.
✓ Communicate your wishes and expectations clearly.	✗ Get bogged down in hours of group photos.

13

Music to Your Ears

One of the most memorable parts of any wedding is the music. Guests will remember if your DJ wore a fish tie or if the band flubbed your first dance much longer than they'll remember whether you served the chicken or salmon. In this chapter, I cover how to find great musicians, what types of bands and DJs to avoid like the plague, and how to treat the talent.

Break It Down

Contrary to popular opinion, you don't want just one group or person to handle your reception music. Sure, you can do it that way, and sometimes having one band or DJ cover everything is the best option. But you should think of the music during your reception as having stages.

Cocktail Music, Anyone?

The first stage is the cocktail music when guests enter your reception. Don't cut corners and decide not to have any music during the cocktail hour. Even if you just have the keyboardist from the band play piano or your DJ pipe background music into the room, guests should be greeted by some sound when they arrive.

The cocktail hour is a great time to have some fun with the music. If you played classical music during the ceremony, now is a great time to change pace. I've had brides select island music for the cocktail hour because they were heading to the Caribbean for their honeymoon or an Irish band to represent their heritage. Don't be afraid to do something totally different for this part of the reception. After all, it's only about an hour so you don't have to worry about people getting sick of an entire night of reggae.

DON'T Forget Logistics

You might be tempted to have the same string quartet play for your ceremony and your reception, but think through the timing before you sign them up for both. If the ceremony and reception aren't in the same space, your musicians will have to pack up and drive from one location to another, unpack, and set up again before they can play a single note. By this time, your guests will have certainly arrived at the reception—to no music.

Music to Dine By

Traditionally, the band or DJ plays music while your guests are eating. It's best to keep the music instrumental and at a very low volume at this point. One of the most frequent complaints I hear about wedding music is that it's too loud to talk over. The meal service can be a great time to give your band a break and serve them dinner as well. This way you can save them for when guests are ready to dance. Have the band play background music on CD or ask a few band members to play at a time and rotate during the meal service.

Another option for dinner music is to have a separate group play while guests dine. Usually classical music works best at this time because it is soft and nonvocal. Strolling violinists can be a nice touch. For a dramatic effect, I've had violinists create a pathway as guests came into the ballroom. They continue to play throughout the dinner. Whether you use your band or a separate group, keep the music low so guests can actually hear each other.

Get on the Bandwagon

If nothing but a live band will do for your wedding, you now have the task of finding the perfect band that can play the swing music your parents love, the Motown your fiancé wants, and crank it up with some contemporary dance music late in the evening for your girlfriends. Easier said than done.

DO Start Early

Great bands book up fast, so if you intend to have a band at your wedding reception, don't put off hiring one for very long. Try to tackle this pretty soon after you have your wedding date and sites locked in. Otherwise, don't come crying to me when you're stuck with a lead singer who wears a green leisure suit.

First, you need to determine the type of band you're looking for. Bands today specialize in everything from zydeco to big band to '80s cover hits, as well as traditional wedding bands that play a little bit of everything.

Determining Your Wedding Music Style

○ What music do you love, and what do you hate?

○ What is the age range of your guests? Try to take all your guests into consideration.

○ Are your guests dancers? Be honest with yourself. If your crowd is more interested in conversation, don't book an energetic dance band and have an empty dance floor.

○ What's the style of your reception, and what's the time of day? Don't expect people to get down to heavy R&B at a daytime wedding unless you have a very die-hard crowd.

143

○ Do you have cultural or ethnic music needs? Most bands can play the one or two favorite ethnic tunes, but if half of your guests will be flying over from Ireland, you may want to book a group with a wider repertoire.

Variety wedding bands can be a great option because they cover a wide range of music that spans all ages. They won't be experts at everything, though. If you have your heart set on hearing top-notch Motown music, you'd be better off hiring a band that specializes in Motown.

Test-Driving the Talent

Yes, it's true that the best way to select a band is to hear them perform, but be very careful about crashing other weddings in your search for the dream group. Some band agents won't let you do it (and would you really want dozens of couples crashing your wedding to hear the band?), and others only agree if the bride and groom give permission. If you are allowed to stop by another event to hear a band, please don't wear jeans and belly up to the bar for a drink. Dress appropriately, and be as inconspicuous as humanly possible.

If you can't see the bands you're considering in person, try to get DVDs or videotapes of them to watch. Be warned that these tapes are never as good as the band is in person, so don't get too discouraged if you think each tape is cheesier than the last. I often tell brides and grooms to listen to the tape without watching first so they won't get distracted by the fog machines or dance moves. Keep in mind that these tapes are made to appeal to a wide range of events, from corporate parties to bar mitzvahs to weddings, so they may not be tailored to weddings. You do get some say as to how your band dresses and performs, so don't toss out a band because you hate the lead singer's outfit.

Once you've found a band you love, you should ask a few questions before plunking down your deposit.

Music to Your Ears

Questions to Ask a Band Before Signing On

○ How many members are in the band? Are horn sections an extra option?

○ Are the musicians on the tape or DVD still in the band? (Be sure the same group will be at your wedding!)

○ Can they do continuous music or will they require breaks? How long are the breaks, and will they supply the break music CDs?

○ What is the band's attire? Can you make requests regarding the dress?

○ What is the overtime fee?

○ How far in advance do they need to set up? If you need them to be set up early, what's the extra charge?

○ Who acts as the MC?

○ Will they learn a song or two for your wedding? How much lead time do they need?

○ Can they play any important cultural songs such as the hora?

○ Do they have a sound system to play CDs if you want to provide break music?

After you've found a band you like, asked all the right questions, and are ready to lock in your dream band, request a contract. Be sure you specify things in the contract such as overtime, extra fees, and continuous music. Mention band members by name if they are the reason you selected the band.

DO **Keep an Eye on the Clock When Band-Shopping**
Although it's important to check out several bands until
you find one you like, remember that good bands get
snapped up quickly. While you're spending weeks trying to hear
all your options in person, you might be losing out on the band you
really want.

DJs: The Good, the Bad, and the Ugly

You've decided that the only way to do your favorite songs justice is
by hiring a DJ. This can often be a great option and can save you
bundles of cash, too. DJs today are a much more polished and professional bunch (for the most part) than they used to be, and I always
recommend hiring a great DJ over a mediocre band.

Scouting Out a DJ

How do you find a really great DJ and avoid the cheesy ones in blue
tuxedos? Word of mouth is the best way. Ask wedding vendors, your
reception site or hotel, and any recent brides you trust. I always recommend talking to the DJs on the phone or meeting with them in person.
Occasionally, you can stop by an event and see them in action, but be
sure to observe the same protocol you would when checking out a band.

Questions to Ask Potential DJs

○ How much do they talk during the reception? (Be specific on
how interactive you want your DJ to be.)

○ Do they serve as the MC, or do they require a separate person to make announcements?

146

○ Are they willing to obtain any of your favorite songs they don't own? Let the DJ know your favorite types of music, and ask to see his selections.

○ What do they wear? If the wedding is black tie, tell them.

○ How new is their equipment? (You don't want to be surprised by ratty speakers on your wedding day.)

○ How frequently do they perform at weddings? You want a DJ who knows how to run a wedding, not one who is used to mixing records at a nightclub.

You're the Boss

When it comes to hiring a DJ, personality is a huge factor. Be sure you click with the person and you feel they are listening to you. If someone comes across as bossy or abrasive when you speak with them, cross them off your list pronto. A good DJ needs to tailor his performance to your needs, not try to convince you that "The Electric Slide" is a crowd-pleaser even though you've listed it on your "don't play" list.

The best way to ensure that your reception is a success is to provide as much direction to your DJ as possible. I'm not saying to tie their hands so they can't actually do their job, but give them enough information so they understand the style of your wedding and how you want the party to progress.

Information to Give Your DJ

○ A list of songs you'd love to hear and, more important, a list of songs they shouldn't play under pain of death.

○ The order of announcements with phonetic spellings of any tricky names. Be sure to review these again right before the reception.

○ The wedding day schedule that outlines how the event will flow, including the timing of the meal service and all the special events.

○ The name of their on-site contact. The DJ will need to communicate with the on-site coordinator or banquet captain so he doesn't announce toasts before the champagne has been poured.

Taking Care of the Talent

The best way to get a great performance from your band or DJ is to treat them well. Take the time to think about how to make their jobs more enjoyable, and you'll get musicians who are thrilled to go the extra mile for you. Even the best band loses its passion if the members are treated poorly. Not communicating with your musicians or making lots of last-minute changes also leaves them scrambling to accommodate the needed switches and makes the event more stressful for everyone.

Getting the Most from Musicians

You don't have to give your band or DJ huge wads of cash to look like a superstar. Just by thinking of how to make the evening more comfortable for them will make you stand out among the hundreds of brides and grooms they see each year.

Ways to Make Your Band or DJ Happy

○ Don't be a music dictator. Although it's great to give a "play" and "don't play" list, resist the temptation to plan every song you want the band to play. Give them the flexibility to do their job.

○ Ask for any special needs ahead of time. Check on the size of stage, dressing rooms, and power requirements they'll need before they're walking in the reception site to set up.

○ Arrange for parking if you can. Be sure to give clear directions for load-in and the correct name of the room they'll be playing in (if there's more than one at the reception site).

○ Arrange for meals for the band or DJ. You don't have to spring for filet mignon, but setting up a room for them to relax in with drinks and dinner will show that you thought about them.

Sad Story/Happy Ending

When a hurricane passed through Washington, D.C., a few years ago, it left many parts of the city without power and water. The day after the storm, I had a wedding at a historical house downtown that thankfully had power, but not lots of it. The band required more circuits than were working on the main floor, but they were able to pare down what they needed to the bare minimum so we didn't blow any fuses, and the bride and groom still got their great band. Even though the band didn't have all the bells and whistles they were used to, they were great team players and turned a potentially stressful event into a huge success.

Setting the Rules

Bands (like any other vendors) appreciate clarity, so be sure to give them plenty of information ahead of time. Don't expect them to be thrilled if you hand them a timeline that either doesn't allow for ample breaks or makes the evening a succession of short, choppy dance sets. Talk over the schedule and your expectations at least a week or two prior to the event to give you both enough time to work out any glitches.

Info to Share with Your Band Before the Reception

○ **Your preferences on drinking.** If you don't want the band drinking at your wedding, let them know.

○ **Your feelings about signage.** If you don't like the idea of the band's name in neon, tell them you'd prefer they leave the signs at home.

○ **Breaks.** Discuss how many, when, and where they can take breaks. Let them know if you're providing a meal for them.

○ **Announcements.** Give these to the band ahead of time so they have plenty of time to review them to avoid mispronunciations and goofs.

○ **The load-in timing.** Be clear on when you want all the musicians set up and when sound checks should be completed. Nothing is worse than a band testing the sound system next door to your ceremony.

Reception Music

Do	Don't
✓ Consider creative options for cocktail music.	✗ Eliminate cocktail music.
✓ Interview potential bands and DJs.	✗ Hire someone who doesn't listen to you.
✓ Take care of your musicians by planning ahead for their needs.	✗ Forget to communicate expectations and comfort.

14

The Ceremony: Here Comes the Bride

The wedding ceremony is really the heart and soul of your celebration, but sometimes it gets overlooked in all the hoopla over the more glamorous details such as flowers and dresses. Take some time to think about your ceremony now so you don't end up with some slapdash vows and a few hastily chosen readings you won't remember in a few years. In this chapter, I guide you through the process of selecting an officiant, personalizing your ceremony, and creating memorable keepsakes.

Will You Marry Me?

If you're getting married in a house of worship, you won't need to search for someone to perform the ceremony. But if you're holding your ceremony at a hotel or in a garden, you'll need to find someone who can marry you at your location. Keep in mind that some religions don't recognize ceremonies that take place outside of the church, so you might be in for an uphill battle if you want to have a Catholic nuptial mass in your parents' backyard.

Finding the perfect officiant to perform your ceremony can be a daunting task. Hotels and other wedding vendors can be a great source for freelance officiants, as can the Internet. Some churches and synagogues have celebrants who will perform ceremonies outside the church, but not all are open to this.

I have had some brides become so obsessed with what they envision a minister or judge to look like that they lose sight of the main objective. You should not be holding beauty pageant auditions or searching for a grandfatherly minister who "looks the type." You need to evaluate potential ceremony celebrants on more substantial issues.

Questions to Ask Potential Officiants

○ How flexible are they in creating and personalizing a ceremony? If you want a completely secular ceremony, are they comfortable with that?

○ How open are they to multicultural or interfaith ceremonies?

○ What do they wear to perform ceremonies? If your families will feel more comfortable with a robed officiant, be sure this is an option.

○ Do they require a certain number of meetings prior to the wedding?

○ Do they attend and run the rehearsal?

○ How many other weddings will they perform the same day as yours? Popular officiants might be quite booked during May and June, and it's good to know if they'll be hurrying from— or to—another wedding.

○ What are their rules about photography and videography during the ceremony?

○ What is the fee for their services?

It's important that you feel a connection with the person you choose to perform the ceremony and that he or she is willing to listen to your input about the ceremony. It's a good idea for you and your fiancé to meet with the potential officiant more than once so you don't feel like you're being married by a total stranger.

Sad Story/Happy Ending

I had one very sweet Jewish bride who was marrying an equally sweet Protestant boy. Each wanted their heritage evident in the ceremony, but neither was comfortable with a celebrant from the other person's religion. It was getting to be a real stumbling block in the planning process! We ended up finding a nondenominational minister who was extremely flexible and who actually learned many of the Jewish wedding customs to include in the ceremony. He agreed to wear a suit instead of his traditional robes and worked diligently with the couple to create a ceremony that blended both religions. He even conducted a beautiful traditional Jewish ketubah ceremony, and the bride's mother was tickled pink!

The Long or Short of It

If you're getting married in a church or synagogue, the order of the service might be predetermined to a great degree. Depending on the faith, you might have no input or you may be able to select readings and musical selections.

DO Ask First

Be sure you clear the readings and musical selections with your officiant before finalizing things or printing your programs. Don't make any changes to the traditional vows or order of the ceremony without getting it approved first, especially if you're getting married in a church or synagogue. I've heard of brides having to reprint programs because they didn't get the service approved before going to press. Yikes!

Most ceremonies have a similar structure and differ primarily in the personal elements you add or alter. If you're getting married outside of a house of worship, you will have much greater flexibility over what you can change.

Ceremony Basics

You may choose to have all these ceremony elements or just pick and choose the ones you like:

- Prelude music
- Processional
- Welcome
- Opening prayer
- Charge to the couple
- Declaration of consent
- Scripture readings
- Vows
- Ceremony of rings
- Kiddush cup (for Jewish ceremonies)
- Seven Blessings (for Jewish ceremonies)
- Reading of the Ketubah (for Jewish ceremonies)
- Pronouncement of marriage
- Closing prayer
- Presentation of couple
- Breaking of the glass (for Jewish ceremonies)
- Recessional

Customize Your Wedding ... Without Making People Cringe

Some parts of the ceremony are easier to customize than others. Keep in mind that you want to create a ceremony that represents you and your fiancé well, not be so sappy and personal that you make all your guests fidget in their seats.

The Ceremony: Here Comes the Bride

Ceremony Elements to Personalize

○ **The prelude and processional music.** If you aren't in a church setting, you could go with anything from The Beatles to Coldplay. You'd be surprised by how pretty Coldplay is on strings!

○ **Readings.** If you choose to have readings, you can opt for poetry, religious scripture, or even words you've written yourself.

○ **Symbolic rituals.** Unity candles, breaking the glass, jumping the broom, drinking from the kiddush cup and other cultural rituals can be woven into your ceremony.

○ **Vows.** Sometimes even churches allow you to customize the traditional vows. If you're getting married on the beach or the top of a mountain, you pretty much have free rein.

○ **Music during the ceremony.** This is a great time for solos or performances by friends and family members.

Before you get too excited about all the wonderfully creative things you can do to make your ceremony the most unique wedding in the history of the world, step back and assess your style and your fiancé's. Don't overload your ceremony with so many personal touches that the meaning gets lost.

Ceremony Blunders to Avoid

○ Vows that crack a lot of jokes or make inappropriate innuendos.

○ Symbolic ceremonies that don't have any personal significance to you. Using Native American customs in your ceremony may sound great but may come off as odd to your guests if you've never had any connection to the culture before.

○ Performance by the bride and groom. Unless you are trained professionals, you will most likely be too nervous to pull this one off well.

○ Too many readings. Don't try to use every friend you've ever had as a reader in the ceremony. Listening to poetry, no matter how beautiful, for half an hour gets old fast.

○ A hodge-podge of readings, songs, and cultural traditions. Even if your personalities are eclectic, your ceremony should have some cohesion. Don't throw an ancient tea ceremony in with a traditional Jewish ceremony, add a modern jazz saxophone performance, and finish off with Victorian poetry.

A little personalization goes a long way. Make the elements of the ceremony that are meaningful to you stand out by letting them be unique. Don't clutter it up!

Blending Religions

Very few weddings I plan have a bride and groom from the same religious background. I am almost surprised if I have a ceremony in which both participants are Presbyterian or Jewish or Hindu. Sometimes, planning the ceremony is a simple matter of blending two religious backgrounds into one ceremony; other times, it creates more drama than a soap opera.

Tips for Blending Religions in Wedding Ceremonies

○ **Get married on neutral turf.** Instead of choosing one church over another, select a nonreligious site or a nondenominational chapel.

○ **Compromise.** Blending Catholic and Presbyterian? Why not meet somewhere in the middle and find an Episcopal church you both like.

○ **Have two officiants.** Having a representative from each religion take part in conducting the ceremony makes things appear equal.

The Ceremony: Here Comes the Bride

○ **Pull traditions from each religion into the ceremony.** Even if you play "Ave Maria" for the processional, you can still include the Jewish custom of breaking the glass at the end of the ceremony.

○ **Explain yourself.** If you have a number of guests who won't understand the customs you're using in the ceremony, explain them in your program.

If you and your fiancé come from different ethnic backgrounds, you may also want to include parts of each background in your ceremony. Although I have had weddings where couples actually have separate marriage ceremonies for each culture (talk about a long day!), it is entirely possible to combine cultural elements into a single ceremony. Talk with your fiancé and both families about what elements are important for each side to include in the ceremony.

The integration can be subtle. At one Jewish/Chinese ceremony, we wrapped red silk the bride's mother brought from China with the groom's tallis and used both to decorate the chuppah. At an Irish/Mexican ceremony, we had the bride process behind an Irish piper and then at the end of the ceremony we threw open the church doors and mariachis serenaded the couple as they left the church!

DON'T Leave Him Out

Although a wedding is traditionally considered the bride's day, don't make the mistake of excluding your fiancé's religious or cultural background unless it means nothing to him. It's a gracious nod to his family to include customs that will make them feel comfortable. I'll never forget the bride who was so obsessed with having a French-themed wedding (not that she was French, mind you) that she completely ignored the groom's Latin American heritage. Half the wedding guests spoke Spanish, but everything at the wedding, from the ceremony music to the food, was French!

Get With the Program

You've carefully thought out your ceremony, included just enough personal touches to make it memorable, and have had it approved by your officiant. Hooray! Now you just have to decide how you'll present the ceremony to your guests. Although programs are by no means a necessity, they can be a lovely memento as well as a way to clue people in to the traditions they'll be witnessing and introduce the participants. If your ceremony will be extremely brief and simple and guests won't have any reason to feel lost without a program, you can skip this detail.

The Bare Necessities

I've seen brides go hog wild with programs, making them enormous booklets that include every word of the ceremony. This isn't necessary, though. Programs are meant to give guests an idea of what to expect and to serve as a keepsake. They don't need to provide so much reading material that guests can't even finish reading them before the ceremony is over.

Information to Include in Your Ceremony Program

- ○ **The basics.** The names of the bride and groom, the wedding date and time, and the location of the ceremony.

- ○ **The order of service.** This can be a simple list or can include such details as the musical selections and names of readers and readings.

- ○ **The participants.** A list of the family and wedding party.

- ○ **The officiants.** The full names and titles of the people marrying you.

A Memorable Memento

Beyond the basics, you can add lots of touches to make your program personal. From the content to the design, programs can be more than just a glorified church bulletin.

Ways to Pump Up Your Program

○ Have customized artwork on the cover. One kindergarten teacher used a drawing one of her pupils drew of a bride and groom for her program cover. Inexpensive and creative!

○ Include information about your bridal party (how you know each one, for instance).

○ Include a message thanking family and friends for being a part of the day.

○ Include a special poem or quote.

○ If your ceremony includes two different cultures, consider having a bilingual program.

○ Include any interesting history about the ceremony site on the back.

DO **Allow Time**

Don't leave the programs until the last minute. Although you must finalize a lot of details before you can get them printed, allow yourself at least 3 weeks before the wedding to get them turned around. Sure, it can be done faster in a pinch, but you need time to proofread carefully (nothing like having 200 copies of a typo to hand out at your ceremony) and don't want to be holding your breath that the printer will ship them in time for the wedding.

Once you have your perfect programs in hand, be sure to assign someone to hand them out (either the ushers or special friends). It's nice to have them displayed in a pretty basket or cool galvanized buckets. Don't ruin the effect by slapping them on a table and letting guests fend for themselves!

The Ceremony

Do	Don't
✓ Find an officiant who is flexible.	✗ Forget to get your ceremony approved.
✓ Personalize your ceremony carefully.	✗ Mix too much into the ceremony.
✓ Blend your religions and cultures.	✗ Wait too late to print programs.

15

Pulling the Look Together

Although I am a huge proponent of focusing your wedding time and money on the things that will make the biggest impact, I also know the power of details. Often it's the little things that don't cost much that will stick in your guests' memories. This doesn't mean I'm advocating filling your wedding with lots of cheesy, pre-fab wedding accessories, either. In this chapter, I tell you how to pull your wedding look together with well-thought-out details and creative touches, and how to avoid looking like you wiped out a dollar store in desperation.

Let Them Eat Cake

Although the wedding cake can be considered part of your catering and is often considered part of the served meal, it is still a decorative element that should be cohesive with your overall wedding. Wedding cakes have come a long way from the cardboard concoctions of days gone by, and are now expected to be flavorful as well as beautiful.

The Taste Test

You no longer have to have a white cake with white icing to be considered a bona fide bride. You don't even have to have a cake that looks like a cake, but more on that later.

Wedding cakes should be tasty, and tasting cakes is one of the best parts of the planning. Set up meetings with bakers early if the cake is important to you because top bakers can only do one or two cakes per weekend. Find out what flavors the baker offers. If the baker doesn't offer your favorite flavors, mention this. They may be able to create a custom flavor for you.

DO **Balance Flavors**

If you're serving a dessert course at your wedding, try to balance the dessert with your cake. Don't follow a rich chocolate dessert with a rich chocolate cake. If you do want a chocolate cake, consider serving a lighter dessert or a sorbet.

Dessert Design

If you've found photos of cakes you love the look of in books or magazines, take them along when you meet with bakers. Even if you only like certain elements from a cake, most bakers can combine looks to create the perfect customized cake for you. Think about whether you prefer the smooth look of fondant icing or the rich taste of buttercream icing and what type of décor you're drawn to. Certain designs will work better on fondant and others will be better for butter cream.

Creative Cake Ideas

○ For large weddings, display a cake to serve half or three quarters of the guests and then have sheet cakes in the kitchen to make up the rest. No one will be any wiser!

○ Have a cupcake cake displayed on stacked tiers.

○ Serve a groom's cake along with your wedding cake. This can be a funky design and is usually a more exotic or rich flavor than the bride's cake.

○ Serve a *crocembouche,* the French wedding cake that's a tower made of stacked profiteroles (cream puffs to you and me) and covered in spun sugar, a sugar syrup, or even chocolate sauce.

○ If you'll be having a lavish dessert display with the cake, you can have a smaller cake because guests will fill up on other treats as well.

○ Use a vintage wedding topper to adorn your cake. Retro toppers can be so kitch that they're cute!

○ If your reception is a smaller affair, serve individual wedding cakes to your guests.

Sad Story/Happy Ending

A butter-cream icing for an outdoor wedding in July is a bad idea unless you like the idea of your wedding cake melting and collapsing in front of your eyes. During one wedding, the air conditioning in a historic home broke. I noticed that the wedding cake was beginning to sink so we quickly moved up the cake cutting so we wouldn't have wedding cake all over the floor. No one ever knew the cake almost didn't make it!

Do Me a Favor

Brides seem to spend an inordinate amount of time worrying about favors, especially considering the fact that most guests either devour them in 2 seconds or leave them behind at the end of the night. I always tell brides that favors can be wonderful if they are something that has unique meaning to you or is a personal reflection of you and your fiancé. Otherwise they're just meaningless trinkets that take up room on your reception tables.

Something Sweet

If you must have a favor because it is the thing to do where you live and guests will expect something, you can't go wrong with something for guests to eat. The traditional wedding favor in many cultures is Jordan almonds—almonds covered in sugar and in various colors. If this is a die-hard wedding tradition in your family, then by all means include it in your wedding. If you're looking for an inexpensive out for favors, though, please skip it. I can't tell you how many Jordan almonds I've thrown away at the end of an evening because they just aren't the easiest or tastiest thing to eat.

Creative Food Favors

○ A bag of the bride's or groom's favorite cookies with the recipe printed on a card for guests to take.

○ An interactive candy bar. Fill glass apothecary jars with all sorts of favorite candies (all white candies make for a great look) and let guests fill their own bags or boxes to take home.

○ A box of *petits fours* (small iced and decorated cake pieces) decorated in the wedding colors.

○ A miniature version of the wedding cake boxed up for each guest. Clearly, this is not an option for brides on a budget!

○ Jordan almonds tucked in tiny bird nests for an outdoor wedding.

○ Color-coordinated ice-cream sandwiches in the shape of hearts wrapped in cellophane. Perfect for a summer wedding!

○ Breakfast to go. For a wedding that ends in the wee hours of the morning, send your guests off with bags of donuts or bagels for the morning. Individual boxes of Krispy Kreme donuts are a huge hit!

Pulling the Look Together

The more creative your edible favor is, the more guests will remember it. It doesn't necessarily cost more to come up with a fun idea that sets your wedding favor apart from all the rest, even if it does get devoured in a matter of minutes.

Something to Take

If you'd rather select a favor that will be a keepsake of the wedding, try to put yourself in your guests' shoes. Would you really want to walk around with a keychain that has someone else's names and wedding date on it? I know I wouldn't.

DON'T Confuse Your Wedding with the Prom

Stay away from any type of favor you can get out of a catalog that also sells castle backdrops for high school dances. Frosted wine glasses that have your names engraved on them are best suited for prom, not your wedding. Avoid such prefab favors like the plague.

Creative Keepsake Ideas

❍ Personalized bottles of champagne or wine.

❍ Place card holders. One Chinese bride used silver place card holders in the shape of fortune cookies.

❍ Picture frames. If you don't put your names on these, guests can reuse them.

❍ CDs with your favorite songs.

❍ Digital portraits. Have guests' pictures taken when they arrive and then send them home with a print.

Doing Double-Duty

The best way to incorporate a favor into the wedding without breaking the bank is to have it perform two functions. One of the most common ways to do this is to have your escort cards (cards that indicate at which tables guests will sit) also be your favor. You can also design your table centerpieces so they break away into several smaller components that can be taken as favors.

Favor Double-Duty Ideas

○ Have the flowers used at the wedding tied into small bouquets for ladies to take as they leave. (This requires some additional staff and some logistical maneuvering.)

○ Have a votive candle with each guest's name on it at their place. This tells them where to sit, and they can take the candle with them when they depart.

○ Tie tags around splits of champagne (small, individual-size champagne bottles) with each guest's name and table assignment, and display them in alphabetical order on the escort card table.

○ Use tiny botanical garden stakes with each guest's name and table, and display them on a table covered in wheat grass.

○ Make customized CD covers with each guest's name and table number on them, and display them in lieu of escort cards.

The Little Extras

Before I even begin to talk about all the extra things you can include in your wedding, I have to warn you to proceed with caution. Creative touches can absolutely make the wedding when they're done cohesively and with a light touch, but they can also become over-the-top very easily if they aren't thought through. It is a slippery slope from "cute as a button" to "what was she thinking?"

DON'T Overdo It

Although you might love the idea of having a guestbook in which guests paste Polaroid pictures *and* the concept of guests writing wishes on note cards and dropping them into a glass bowl, you need to pick one or the other. Incorporating every cute idea that ever graced the pages of *Martha Stewart Weddings* into your wedding is not creative; it is overwhelming and will make you look like you couldn't make a decision. Use fun ideas sparingly and only if you really love them. I've seen weddings where the bride got so carried away with all—and I do mean *all*—the fun details she'd been ripping out of magazines that her reception ended up looking like a carnival of good ideas gone wrong.

Escort Cards or Place Cards?

First let's define the terms: *escort cards* tell a guest which table they're seated at, and *place cards* assign an actual seat at the table. If you're serving a seated meal, you'll want to have assigned tables for your guests at the least. Open seating never works as well as people envision it will. There are always a few couples wandering around trying to locate open seats and only finding an odd chair here or there. Save your guests the trouble, and assign tables.

Whether to use place cards at the guest tables is a matter of personal preference. Some brides like to decide who their guests will spend the evening talking to, and others prefer to forgo the hassle and let guests seat themselves. If you do decide to assign seats at the tables, leave yourself time at the end of the planning. It isn't always an easy task.

DO Use Envelopes

Save yourself some hassle by using envelope-style escort cards instead of the tent variety. This way you can write the name of the guest on the outside of the card and the table number on the inside. When you need to make last-minute changes to the seating (which you will), all you have to do is switch the inserts. No rewriting names or crossing out table numbers. It isn't a bad idea to get some extra inserts printed to make the switching easier.

What's on the Menu?

Having menu cards on the tables in a nice touch and one that doesn't have to be expensive. Instead of having cards printed for each guest, just have two or three at each table. Or print them yourself and put one or two in a lovely frame at each table.

Menu cards can also do double-duty as place cards if you have a calligrapher write each guest's name at the top of the menu and tuck it into their napkin. This turns your menu card into a nice keepsake as well.

If you're serving a buffet or stations, you may have menu cards at the table so guests don't miss anything. Some guests may not even realize there are different options at different stations if you don't inform them! Another option is to print larger menu cards and place them in frames on the buffet or at each station.

You can also do "menu" cards for the bar if you're serving specialty drinks. Printing descriptions of the drinks and framing them makes for inexpensive bar décor and reminds guests of the tasty concoctions.

Guest Books You'll Look at Again

If you want a guest book, try some of the following unique options and skip the traditional bow-festooned book that will get shoved in the back of a drawer, never to be seen again.

DO Provide Lots of Opportunity

I never recommend displaying the guest book prior to the ceremony, because it creates a traffic jam as everyone arrives at the same time and waits to sign the book. Instead, display the book during the cocktail hour in a heavily trafficked area or near the escort cards. Then you can move the book to another location during dinner so guests will pass by it frequently, and move it near the exit as guests depart so no one misses a chance to sign it.

Unique Guest Book Alternatives

○ Individual note cards for guests to write you a wedding wish or piece of wedding advice.

○ Small blank books at each table for guests to pass around and write messages. You can even include questions or ideas for guests to write about.

○ A lovely coffee table book featuring the city you're getting married in or a favorite topic. Provide metallic paint pens so guests can write on the photos and you can display it in your home.

○ Have guests sign a silver tray with an etching pen.

○ Have guests sign a tablecloth or a runner with a fabric pen.

○ Assign friends to take Polaroid pictures of guests as they arrive and then have the guests sign the photos and paste them in an album.

○ Frame an engagement photo with a large, blank mat and have guests sign the mat. After the wedding, you can substitute a wedding photo and hang it in your home with all your guests' signatures and messages.

Powder Rooms with Pizzazz

If your reception is in a space with dreary or utilitarian restrooms, it's nice to dress up that space as well. Usually I recommend focusing attention on the ladies' room. Men just don't care as much about scented candles.

If your reception site restroom has brown paper towels on a roll the size of a wheel of cheese, consider bringing in pretty hand towels—you can even have them monogrammed if you so desire. Have your florist provide a small vase of flowers and light a few candles to make the space more inviting. An amenity basket stocked with everything from mints to safety pins to lip balm is always appreciated. Get a cute basket, and fill it with travel sizes of all the necessities. These little touches will go a long way in making your guests feel welcome.

Pulling the Look Together

Do	Don't
✓ Personalize your favors.	✗ Do favors just for the sake of doing them.
✓ Have your details do double-duty.	✗ Overdo the creative touches.
✓ Dress up the ladies' room.	✗ Put a guest book out at the ceremony.

16

Get Me to the Church on Time

Certainly one of the least exciting and glamorous parts of the wedding day is the transportation. Not that arriving in a stylish antique car or an elegant horse-drawn carriage isn't fabulous, but there's a lot more to moving people on your wedding day than your grand entrance. In this chapter, I give you the nitty-gritty on finding the perfect way to arrive in style, and how to make sure you don't get left in the dust!

Planes, Trains, and Automobiles

Okay, so you probably won't arrive to your wedding by plane (I strongly discourage skydiving as a method of transportation), but you have lots of options when it comes to getting around on your wedding day. The first thing you need to consider when you start thinking about transportation in general is how involved you want to get.

How Much Is Enough?

Most brides don't think about this part of the planning until the very end (after they've done all the fun and creative stuff), when their budget is already stretched to the max. Unfortunately, transportation is one of those elements that can quickly take a huge bite out of your budget. The moment you start to provide buses for 200 guests, enough limos to move all the bridal party and family, or valet parking, you're talking some serious dough.

It's best if you can do an honest assessment of the types of vehicles you really need for your wedding before you rush out and book every limousine in town. Take a look at your guest list and the timing of your wedding day to really get a good idea of what will work best.

Questions to Ask Yourself About Transportation

○ Are most of your guests from out of town? Will most be without cars?

○ Do you have a good number of elderly or handicapped guests?

○ Are your ceremony and reception in different locations?

○ Are taxis difficult to come by where you're getting married (consider what happens if it rains, too), or are they not even an option?

○ Are the hotels you've selected for your guests far away from the ceremony and reception?

○ Are any major events taking place the day of your wedding that might block traffic?

○ Is parking at your ceremony or reception site difficult or nonexistent?

If you find yourself saying "yes" to any of these questions, you should seriously consider arranging transportation for your guests to and from your wedding. Although it can be expensive to move all your guests, consider the horror of having more than 100 people trying to hail cabs in a rain storm. Guests won't remember what you served or how gorgeous your centerpieces were if they end up being an hour late to the reception—and soaking wet!

If you have a much simpler scenario for your wedding, you may be able to get away with just providing transportation for the bridal party and family. But even if your wedding guests are all local, it's nice to get your attendants to and from the wedding. Most brides provide transportation for their bridesmaids, even if they let their groomsmen fend for themselves, but spring for the extra limousine to move all your attendants if you can.

When it comes to family cars, analyze the dynamics of both families to determine the number and types of cars. If you have divorced parents, putting everyone in one limousine might not be the best option. Talk to your families and get their preferences before the wedding day to avoid any last-minute drama.

DO **Think Small**
In some situations, it may be easier to hire a few town cars than one larger limousine. If parents don't get along or you want the groom's family at the church much earlier than yours for photos, it might make sense to get a few sedans. This gives you more flexibility in timing and can often prevent World War III from breaking out.

Arriving in Style

Even if you go simple for the cars that will move your bridal party and guests, you can get creative with the type of vehicle you make your grand entrance and departure in. Depending on your town, you probably have lots of fun options for your wedding day transportation.

Unique Wedding Day Transportation

○ An antique car

○ A stretched modern car such as a Hummer or a Jaguar

○ A convertible or superluxury sports car

○ A tour trolley or cable car

○ A boat (Obviously this only works if you're on the water.)

❍ A horse and carriage

❍ A motorcycle (Only for the bravest brides and only at the end of the night when your hair is already a mess!)

❍ A musician (like a bagpiper or trumpeter) to lead you on a short walk from the ceremony to the reception

Think through the logistics of every option before putting down a deposit. A horse and carriage is a charming option until you have to get on a major highway to get from your ceremony to your reception. Also keep the weather in mind when you opt for any of the more creative modes of transportation. Being in an antique car with "antique air conditioning" in July will likely wilt you in about 2 minutes.

Moving the Masses

If you've decided to provide transportation for all your wedding guests, you have a few options. Ask for all the options your local transportation companies offer, and weigh all your options.

The first, and easiest, is to rent large, coach-style buses that hold about 50 people. With larger buses, you have fewer vehicles to deal with and fewer trips to make. However, they can be more difficult to maneuver down narrow streets and it takes longer to fill them up.

Shuttle buses, which hold about 25 to 30 passengers, are a very popular option for weddings. You can fill them quickly and send them on their way so they can return for more guests (if you're planning on your buses making multiple trips). Not to mention, they're much easier to drive down narrow streets and to park!

Open-air trolleys are popular in the Washington, D.C., area because they look charming and the drivers often give tours as they drive. Keep in mind that some guests may not be thrilled to be riding in an open-air bus if it's a scorching day or it's very windy or rainy.

DON'T **Do Too Much Double-Duty**

One of the common transportation goofs brides make is expecting a bus to be able to make more trips than is logistically possible. Always factor in heavy traffic and late guests when you're calculating how many trips one bus can make from the hotel to the church and back again. It always takes longer than you expect. It's not fun to have to start a wedding 20 minutes late because a large chunk of the guests were on the last bus trip.

Dollars and Sense

Transportation logistics can be one of the more frustrating and boring parts of the whole planning process, but you need to pay attention to these details. Be sure to get all your agreements in writing and read them carefully.

The Fine Print

Not all limousine companies are created equal, so the more you spell out ahead of time, the happier you will be on your wedding day. Also, don't be afraid to ask questions or ask to see the vehicles you'll be using before you sign on the dotted line.

Questions to Ask a Transportation Company

○ How old are your cars?

○ How many passengers will they hold comfortably? (If you have large groomsmen, be sure to mention this.)

○ How are the cars laid out inside?

○ What do your drivers wear?

○ What is your cancellation policy?

○ What is your backup if a car breaks down?

○ What amenities are included in the package?

○ Will your drivers provide champagne if requested?

○ How much is overtime, and is it available?

Sad Story/Happy Ending

One very stubborn groom insisted that he and his bride would be ready to leave the reception more than an hour before it ended and booked his get-away car for this departure time, refusing to plan any cushion time into the plans. Of course, when the magic hour rolled around and the car idled out front, he wasn't ready to leave. Unfortunately, the limousine had another job and after waiting an hour, the driver had to leave. I was able to get another car by the time the groom meandered outside, but not without a great deal of stress.

Don't assume you can run over your contracted time. If you think there's any chance you'll be late, put a cushion into your contract, or you might be stranded on the side of the road!

Stretch Your Transportation Budget

There are smart ways to get the most out of your transportation budget, and there are really foolish ways as well. Transportation is one of the areas where brides try to cut back the most often and end up making their wedding a disaster.

Transportation Mistakes to Avoid

○ Not having enough buses to move all your guests to the reception. This happens often when buses make several trips to get guests to the ceremony. Although guests can arrive in a staggered fashion before the ceremony, they all come out of the church at the same time!

Get Me to the Church on Time

- ○ Not having a rain plan if you intend to have a musician lead your guests from the ceremony to the reception.

- ○ Not informing your guests that taxis will be difficult to get at the end of the night.

- ○ Not providing information on where and when transportation will depart. (This is good information to give the guest's hotels as well.)

- ○ Using one limousine to make two trips to get the bridesmaids and groomsmen to the ceremony and then not being able to fit everyone in *after* the ceremony.

- ○ Not getting a car for just you and your groom to take you from the ceremony to the reception. You will appreciate those few private moments before the madness begins again.

- ○ Having the bridal party arrive at the reception way before the bride and groom and then making them wait to be announced. Time the transportation to keep everyone together if you don't want folks wandering off.

There's good news, though: you can cut back on costs for moving people. Hiring fewer (and larger) buses is more cost-effective than getting lots of smaller shuttles (and you'll have fewer drivers to tip, as well). Using larger limousines (such as the superstretch cars that hold 15 or more people) to move your bridal party also saves over multiple limousines. Putting your parents with the bridal party can work well if you don't have a ton of attendants. You can also save some money by using a simpler car such as a sedan to pick you up at the end of the evening, especially if you don't plan a grand exit.

DON'T Assume You Will Get a Break During a Break

Even if you won't be using a car or bus for a few hours, it will probably cost the same to have it return than it would to keep it on-site the whole time. Companies just can't book other jobs during this time, so expect to pay a transfer fee that's higher than additional hours or a new minimum charge for having a car return at the end of the night.

Timing and Traffic

It's important that you plan out your transportation timing and work this into your overall wedding day timeline. Test-drive your routes so you know how much time to allot when you're scheduling multiple trips by one car. This is also important if you're providing directions to guests who are driving to your wedding. Don't rely on maps and computers to give you the most reliable directions. Always drive the directions yourself and make notes of any landmarks along the way. Your guests will thank you for it!

Give a very detailed route with pick-up and departure times to the transportation company ahead of time. If you can fit it into the budget, have a supervisor from the company on-site to oversee the timing. This is especially helpful if you have lots of cars and buses. If you can't hire someone from the company, assign a very detail-oriented friend or family member to be sure the guests know where to get on the buses and to let the driver know when to leave. If all else fails, give detailed instructions to the drivers about when they should leave and the names of any important guests to double-check for. Tell important guests such as ceremony participants and extended family members to be on an early bus.

Transportation

Do	Don't
✓ Consider creative options.	✗ Forget your guests' comfort.
✓ Have back-up plans.	✗ Be afraid to ask questions.
✓ Test-drive directions.	✗ Leave logistics to chance.

17

Staying Cool Under Pressure

This chapter just might be the most important one in the book if you can take away even one kernel of information to help you plan for potential problems, keep everyone in the information loop, and stay sane. In this chapter, I tell you essentially how to be your own wedding coordinator, if you don't choose to hire one!

The Countdown

After you've locked in all your major wedding vendors, chosen your menu, and mailed your invitations, you may be wondering, *Now what?* You've done the hard part, right? Well, yes and no.

It's the Little Things That Count

Some brides find that taking care of all the little details leading up to the wedding is more time-consuming than doing all the major planning. Usually that's because it becomes much harder to assign these tasks to other people. Unfortunately, perhaps, no one can select your first dance song but you and your fiancé (as much as you might like to give away that task!).

Final Wedding Planning Details to Remember

○ Assign guests to tables and write out escort cards (and place cards, if you wish).

○ Make an alphabetical list of guests and their table assignments, as well as a table-by-table list of names. Give this to your caterer or wedding planner.

○ Purchase your wedding bands (and have them engraved if you like).

○ Select gifts for your wedding party, and write personal notes.

○ Purchase any accessories you'll need: cake knife, toasting flutes, guest book and pen, unity candle, ring bearer's pillow, etc.

○ Make your list of "must-have" shots for your photographer.

○ Learn how to bustle your gown at your final fitting at the salon, and bring along your mother or a bridesmaid to also learn how.

○ Purchase all your personal wedding accessories such as shoes, jewelry, lingerie, stockings, etc. before your fittings so you can try them on with the gown. Your heel height and bra can influence the fit of the gown, so bring them to all your fittings.

○ Give your list of favorite songs and songs not to be played to your band or DJ.

○ Give the final number of centerpieces, corsages, and boutonnieres to your florist 2 weeks before your wedding.

○ Give your final guest count to your caterer the week before the wedding.

Try not to leave all these details to the last week before the wedding. The last thing you want to be doing in the days leading up to your wedding is running around like a chicken with its head cut off.

What You Absolutely Can't Forget

Aside from the myriad details that can consume your mind, you'll need to think through the logistical nitty-gritty of your event several weeks before the big day. This means you have to think like a wedding planner and anticipate all the potential problems that could arise on your wedding day.

Logistics to Remember

○ **Power requirements.** Be sure you know from your band, photographer, videographer, caterer, lighting designer, and even florist what their power requirements are for the wedding. Check with your site to be sure it's wired for it all, or you may need to bring in a generator or scale back on some of the disco lights.

○ **Permits and licenses.** Check with your site and caterer to be sure they both have the proper permits and licenses for the wedding. If you're doing photos at a state or national park site, be sure you have the proper permits, or you may get kicked out!

○ **Insurance.** Check that your vendors have liability insurance (especially your caterer), and consider investing in a one-day event policy to cover you in case a guest falls and decides to sue.

○ **Handicapped access.** If you will have guests who will be in wheelchairs, be sure to plan ahead. Let them know if there are stairs at the sites, and plan on having some ushers to assist any elderly guests who need an extra hand.

○ **The marriage license.** Give yourself plenty of time to get this, especially if your state requires blood tests or waiting periods. Also, don't forget to bring it to the ceremony!

○ **Final payments.** Check all your contracts a month prior to your wedding, and write out all the final checks. Some payments will be required prior to the wedding day, so mail those in plenty of time to arrive. If checks are due on the day of the wedding and you want to wait until then to give them, go ahead and write them out and give them to the best man or another responsible attendant (or family member) to distribute for you.

○ **Gratuity.** If you can include gratuity in the final payments for your vendors, save yourself some hassle and do it then. If not, put cash in labeled envelopes and give them to your official cashier to distribute at the end of the wedding. You don't want to have to hunt for cash at the end of the night!

Rehearse It

Most wedding rehearsals are little better than slightly organized chaos. Believe me, I've run many I felt were on the verge of turning into cocktail parties. In this section, I give you some professional tips to help you run your rehearsal like a wedding planner and get you quickly on your way to the fun part.

DON'T Pack in Too Much

Brides are notorious for setting appointments at the hair salon right before the rehearsal and then running in late because the stylist ran behind. Give yourself lots of time, and don't try to squeeze too much into the last day. Everything should be done by this point, so give yourself time to relax and be on time. It's hard (but not impossible) to run a wedding rehearsal without the bride!

Tips for a Smooth Wedding Rehearsal

○ Expect everyone to be late. If you really need to get started a 6 o'clock, tell your bridal party you're starting at 5:45. Even then you'll get stragglers.

○ Have all ceremony participants attend so your readers are comfortable with microphones.

Staying Cool Under Pressure

○ Don't expect your musicians to attend unless you pay them extra to come. Professionals won't need to rehearse, but they will need someone to give them their cues on the wedding day. If you haven't hired a wedding coordinator, assign someone who can help with the processional and music cues on the wedding day.

○ Bring extra copies of all the readings, and have extras on the wedding day as well.

○ Decide on the order of the processional ahead of time. This will save lots of unnecessary people-shuffling.

○ Let your officiant run the show, especially if you are in his or her church. Your wedding coordinator or friends who are helping you should take a backseat role.

○ Bring copies of the programs.

○ Review the location of where both bridesmaids and groomsmen will enter and wait, as well as the location of restrooms.

○ Be sure everyone knows what time they need to be ready on the wedding day, when they begin photos, and where they should meet to get in limos to go to the wedding ceremony (or what time they should be at the ceremony site if limos aren't provided).

The more organized you are for the wedding rehearsal, the faster and smoother it will run. Once all the players are in attendance, the entire process shouldn't take more than half an hour to 45 minutes.

Remember that this is just a rehearsal to make everyone more at ease with the ceremony. You aren't choreographing a Vegas show, so don't get too caught up in making it look perfect. Even if someone goofs up, the chances are slim any of your guests will even notice.

Timing Is Everything

The most crucial document involving your wedding isn't a contract or even a permit. It's the wedding day schedule. You will create this very detailed timeline of the wedding day to give your vendors. The wedding day schedule outlines the flow of the day from the time the first delivery truck rolls up to when the rice is thrown at the end of the night. If this document is thorough, it should anticipate every contingency and make the day run like clockwork.

DON'T Underestimate

If you choose to have a receiving line (insert audible groan) after the ceremony or during your cocktail hour, remember that it will eat up a lot of time. At a 200-person wedding, it would take you more than 45 minutes to greet everyone if you only spent 15 seconds with each person. Yikes! A better alternative is to visit tables during dinner (after you grab a bite) and say hello to your guests.

Go with the Flow

Although I like to make my schedules very detailed, the purpose isn't to make the day stiff but to plan ahead so it moves naturally from event to event. The more detailed the schedule is, the more the day has been thought through. Surprisingly, this makes everything run seamlessly instead of making it seem forced and controlled.

How to Make a Wedding Schedule

○ The first page should be the point of contact information for everyone involved in your wedding. This includes addresses for all the locations involved and cell phone numbers for everyone you've hired. Get the names of the people who will be making the actual deliveries on your wedding day.

Staying Cool Under Pressure

○ Start the framework of the schedule by plugging in times of the ceremony, reception, photo sessions, dinner service, special dances, cake cutting, toasts, etc.

○ Include the names of all people giving toasts and everyone involved in special dances.

○ Include the timing of all transportation and the routes of each vehicle.

○ Include the timing for hair and makeup and drop-dead ready times.

○ Include the timing and flow of the ceremony with the names of ceremony songs and the order of the processional. Include the names of ushers who will seat each mother or grandmother, as well as which row they will sit in.

○ Include the delivery times for flowers and cake, as well as the arrival and setup times of the caterer, band, photographer, and videographer.

○ Include a list of items to be displayed at each location (guest book, escort cards, favors, etc.) and who will set them up.

○ Include the band breaks and time for your vendors to eat.

When you have a rough draft of your wedding day schedule, send it to your vendors. Ask them for their suggestions. Often the caterer or band will have ideas that may make the evening flow better. Incorporate their suggestions into the final version, and send copies to everyone involved in your wedding. I sometimes highlight each vendor's part to make it easier to navigate, or e-mail it so they can pare it down to the information vital for them.

DO **Give Your Ceremony Participants the Scoop**

It's a great idea to provide copies of the wedding day schedule to your family, bridal party, and readers at the rehearsal. This way everyone is clear on the timing and where they need to be when. You don't have to include all the details your vendors need, though. Make an abridged version that just includes the information your family and bridal party will find useful.

This Is Not Your Mother's Wedding

Before you start plugging every wedding ritual known to man into your wedding schedule, take a moment to think about what you really want to include in your wedding day. Weddings have changed dramatically, and you are no longer obligated to have a bouquet toss or a father/daughter dance if these traditions don't work for you. I've had brides skip cutting the wedding cake (and skip having a cake altogether), nix the garter toss, and forgo a grand exit to stay with their guests until the bitter end.

Customize your wedding schedule to fit your wedding and your personalities. If you're untraditional, don't try to wedge yourself into someone else's preconceived idea of what a wedding reception should be. If you despise the idea of throwing your bouquet, don't let anyone bully you into doing it. There are very few things you absolutely *must* do during a wedding reception anymore, so pick and choose what traditions suit you.

The Wedding Day

A successful wedding day comes down to two things: being prepared and having a good attitude. If you don't think ahead and prepare for potential disasters, you could end up with a mess on your hands and no way to fix it. On the other hand, your wedding can be technically flawless but you can obsess and worry to the point where the only thing your guests notice is your stress.

DO **Try Alternative Traditions**

Brides have gotten creative over the past few years. Instead of tossing a bouquet, you may choose to give your bouquet to a mother, grandmother, or sister at a special moment. I've seen brides dance with their mother when their father was deceased and dance with both a biological father and stepfather during the father/daughter dance. Don't be afraid to step out of the box!

Wedding 911

When it comes to a wedding, the potential for disaster is pretty great. I've seen grooms rip their tuxedos, brides get grease on their dresses, and groomsmen crush their boutonnieres. Believe me, it pays to be prepared for your wedding day with an emergency kit. My kit contains almost anything you could need to fix a wedding day disaster and has gotten me through lots of crises. Plan to stock at least the bare essentials in a bag and give it to your mother or a bridesmaid to take care of.

What to Stock in a Wedding Day Emergency Kit

- Extra pantyhose
- Bobby pins, safety pins, straight pins, and corsage pins
- Fake rings (for the ring bearer's pillow or an emergency)
- Clear nail polish and nail files
- Band-aids
- Breath mints and cough drops
- Butane lighter and matches
- Dental floss
- Comb, brush, and hairspray
- Floral tape
- Scissors
- Scotch tape, masking tape, clear packing tape, and black tape
- Spot remover and static guard
- Super glue
- Visine
- Kleenex

- Q-tips, makeup sponges, and cotton balls
- Rubber bands
- Pocket mirror
- Pressed face powder, water-proof mascara, lipstick, and lip gloss
- White chalk
- Lint brush
- Toothpicks
- Aspirin, Pepto Bismol, and Pepcid AC
- White string, white ribbon, and ivory ribbon
- White-Out
- Moist towelettes
- Tampons and pads
- Ziploc bags
- Mini sewing kit
- Lotion
- Toothpaste

You may not need all these items, but be sure to carry the basics—the pins, sewing kit, breath mints, scissors, stain remover, chalk, and your makeup for touch-ups.

Still worried about a wedding day disaster? Here are some quick fixes for common crises:

- **Stain on your wedding dress?** Try some spot-removing towelettes such as Shout Wipes. If that doesn't work, you can cover the stain on a white dress with chalk or even (in desperate times) White-Out!

- **Groomsman forgot his studs?** Cover the buttons with black tape, and from a distance and in photos, it will look like he is wearing studs.

- **Missing a boutonniere?** Pluck a bloom out of a bridesmaid's bouquet, wrap some green floral tape around the stem, grab a corsage pin from your emergency kit, and you've got an instant boutonniere!

- **Broken boutonniere?** If the flower head has been bent, run a toothpick vertically through the flower head and into the stem to hold it straight.
- **Ripped hem?** Tape it from the underneath with clear packing tape.
- **Rented tux pants too small?** Run a rubber band through the button hole and around the button to keep them together. Your handiwork will likely be hidden under the cummerbund or vest.

Sad Story/Happy Ending

One of my favorite brides stepped into her limousine and got grease all over the front of her gown! Luckily, I had tons of Shout Wipes in my emergency kit, and we scrubbed at the stains until they disappeared. Now I always keep Shout Wipes in my emergency kit. They have saved my neck many times!

Banning Bridezilla

The most important thing to remember on your wedding day is that if you're having a great time and have a relaxed attitude about everything, so will your guests. This is true even if your cake collapses, your limos are late, and a guest spills red wine on your dress. I've seen brides with nearly flawless weddings who are so tense that something will go wrong that they make everyone around them a nervous wreck. On the other hand, I had a bride who was in the emergency room the night before her wedding with severe food poisoning who put on a happy (though slightly pale) face the next day. In both cases, the bride's attitude was contagious, and the weddings took on the mood of the bride.

A successful wedding is *all* about attitude. If you want to ruin your wedding, be sure to micro-manage everyone you hire; be demanding and snippy with your bridesmaids, family, and groom; and nit-pick about every detail of the event. I guarantee the event will be a disastrous flop.

191

Whatever you do, don't let the little things that come up on your wedding day get to you. If possible, assign someone else to handle all the issues on the actual day so you won't even have a chance to worry. (This is where a wedding planner is invaluable.) And if disaster does strike, put on a gracious smile and enjoy the day anyway. When it comes down to it, your wedding is about finding the perfect person, not the perfect centerpiece.

Staying Cool Under Pressure

Do	Don't
✓ Get all permits and licenses early.	✗ Wait until the last minute to take care of the final details.
✓ Be on time to your rehearsal.	✗ Forget to let your vendors review your wedding schedule.
✓ Pack an emergency kit.	✗ Micro-manage on the wedding day.

18

Making a Weekend of It

Destination weddings have become extremely popular over the past few years as a way to extend the wedding celebration beyond just the wedding day and go to an exciting locale. Although destination weddings are becoming more and more mainstream, you need to consider different factors when planning a wedding away than what you'd have to when planning a traditional event. In this chapter, I let you in on the secrets to a successful getaway wedding and what potential pitfalls to avoid.

Getting Away from It All

Destination weddings can be as small as just the bride and groom or as large as a traditional wedding. They're perfect for a couple who want a wedding that's less traditional and usually a lot more relaxed. Getting married on a mountaintop or a beach seems to lend itself to a less-formal atmosphere.

Finding a Spot

Often a bride and groom know exactly the location for their wedding because it is a favorite vacation spot or has special significance (such as where they met or where he proposed). If you don't know exactly where you'd like to get married but know you want a destination wedding, you can still find a perfect place without jetting all over the world.

Tips on Finding a Perfect Destination Locale

○ Check out the real wedding stories on The Knot (www.theknot.
com) and The Wedding Channel (www.weddingchannel.com).
Both sites have great profiles of destination weddings with
info on the locations.

○ Talk to a travel agent who specializes in honeymoons. He or
she should know spots that will be the most amenable to
weddings.

○ Travel magazines and wedding magazines usually list great
honeymoon spots, which are often great wedding spots, too.

○ Surf the web for great destination wedding spots. Lots of
resorts are marketing themselves this way, so you should find
some great options.

Do as much research as possible before committing to a place for
your destination wedding. Try to talk to brides and grooms who have
had weddings at the location you're considering, if possible. It's
always best to get feedback from couples who have had weddings at
the site so you know what worked for them and what didn't.

Considerations When Choosing a Destination Location

○ How difficult is it to get there, and how expensive is travel at
the time of year you're targeting? If guests have to take two
planes and a canoe, you may get a much smaller turnout than
you expected.

○ What will the weather be like? You may get great rates in the
Caribbean in July … but you also may get hurricanes.

○ If you select a particular resort, is it kid-friendly or will guests
need to leave their children at home or find another nearby
option?

Making a Weekend of It

○ Can local florists, musicians, photographers, and cake bakers take care of your wedding, or do things get brought to the island?

○ Do guests need a passport or visas? Are any immunizations required or recommended?

Although you aren't required to pay for your guests' travel and accommodations, it is nice to think about these things when making your plans. Long, expensive flights and pricey resort rates during high season will automatically prohibit some guests from attending. Not that this is always a bad thing. Try to anticipate all the questions your guests will ask, and find answers before you book anything.

Know the Ropes: Foreign Rules and Customs

Aside from thinking about your guests when you choose a spot for a destination wedding, you also should consider the laws that govern weddings. Many countries require a certain length of residency before granting a marriage license to foreigners. In some countries it is only a day or two, but in others it can be more than a month.

Find out what documents are required to apply for the license and if both parties need to be present to apply. Get the address of the courthouse you need to go to as well. Plan ahead so you don't end up without a license because you didn't know all the regulations.

DO Get Help

It's worthwhile hiring a wedding coordinator at the destination you've selected even if just to help coordinate the requirements for the marriage license. She can handle paperwork from her end before you arrive and even take you to the proper places to complete the documents when you arrive. Money well spent!

195

Planning the Long-Distance Wedding

What makes destination weddings so appealing can also make them more challenging. A remote island is an exotic and beautiful place for a wedding, but it doesn't have quite the resources most other places do. Destination weddings work best if you either have an unlimited budget to fly in everything you could possibly want or you are more flexible and willing to compromise so you can get married in an exotic location.

Making the Best of Things

If you are one of those brides who has her heart set on a destination wedding but finds herself challenged by the limited choices, you can still get the most from limited options. First of all, realize that your guests will be much more entranced by the beauty of the backdrop than the décor. With most destination locations, the setting is more beautiful than any hotel ballroom, so play it up!

Tips for Getting the Most from a Little

○ **Keep it simple.** Don't spend weeks trying to hunt down special linens if your resort only has white. You don't want to compete with your setting, anyway.

○ **Use the natural backdrop as much as possible.** Get married overlooking the water so you don't have to worry about any décor but the sunset.

○ **Stick with what's local.** Don't try to fly in tulips from Holland if plenty of gorgeous tropical flowers are locally grown.

○ **Go with specialties.** Serve your guests the local culinary specialties instead of trying to serve a traditional wedding meal of filet and salmon. It's more interesting and will taste much better.

○ **Hire local talent, and let them do what they're best at.** Don't try to force a reggae band to do '50s music.

○ **Bring in small, easily portable details.** You can bring in your own favors, guest book, place cards, and other items that are light and can add a personal touch without weighing down your luggage.

Prioritize your planning, and determine early on if you need to import anything to your destination. You will need to budget ahead for this if it is very important to you. I've planned destination weddings where brides brought photographers with them because they couldn't find what they were looking for at their wedding location. This is an expensive option, so be careful when you start planning to fly in everyone from your hairdresser to your cake baker.

Making the Most of Your Time

When planning a destination event, it is ideal if you can visit the location before your wedding. If at all possible, schedule a site visit a few months before the wedding to meet the people who will be involved on your wedding day or to hire them. If you have wisely hired a wedding coordinator to help you with your long-distance planning, you'll want to meet with her and do the lion's share of the planning during your visit.

What to Do During Your Site Visit

○ Finalize all your wedding vendors and meet with them. Get contracts and put down deposits, if you haven't already.

○ Do a menu tasting for your reception. This may not be standard operating procedure at all places, but at least ask to taste the food.

○ Check out the venues for all your events, and discuss the way the event will be set up.

○ Check out the guest rooms and ask to see the suite you will be staying in.

○ Compile information on extra activities for your guests.

○ Determine the easiest way to get around so you can give this information to your guests. Get numbers of taxi companies and shuttle services.

If you absolutely can't swing a visit to your wedding location ahead of time, plan to arrive a few days early and spend some serious time pulling all the details together. You will have to rely heavily on the local people you have hired and get as much information through them as possible to pass along to your guests.

Setting the Schedule

When most people think of destination weddings, they imagine a series of parties surrounding the wedding instead of just the ceremony and reception. If your guests are traveling a long distance to be with you, it's nice to plan several get-togethers during the time they'll be there. These don't have to be fancy events, but they should be a fun way for your guests to see different parts of the resort you've chosen.

DON'T Be Exclusive

When you have a destination wedding, you should include all your guests at every event (except for a bridesmaid's luncheon, perhaps). Because everyone has spent time and money to travel to be with you, you shouldn't plan on a private rehearsal dinner. The more the merrier!

There are no hard-and-fast rules as to what types of events you should host for your guests or when they should take place, but it is nice to have a welcoming event, whether it be a rehearsal dinner or an earlier event, as well as a farewell event to bookend the wedding.

Don't forget to leave some time in the schedule for guests to do things on their own, as well. It's a nice touch to provide your guests with a list of ideas for activities to do during their free time and information on various local hotspots and sites to see.

Sad Story/Happy Ending

One bride-to-be wanted to plan a full roster of events for her guests while they visited Washington, D.C., for her wedding. We even got tickets for a private tour of the White House through her congressman, which she was sure her guests would be thrilled about. Unfortunately, when her guests found out that the tour started at 7 A.M., they weren't as eager as she was. We ended up having no takers for the special tour! Luckily, the bride finally realized that her guests wanted to explore on their own so she provided maps and guidebooks for everyone and let them wander at will. In the end, everyone was happy doing their own thing.

What Your Guests Need to Know

With a destination wedding, it is crucial to give your guests plenty of information—and give it to them early. If you're asking guests to take vacation days and book airfare and hotel rooms, you can't start the flow of information soon enough. Plan on sending a save-the-date card at least 6 months in advance. This can either be a simple card with bare-bones details or a very complete packet of information. If you go bare bones with the first mailing, you'll need to follow up with more specific details in a second mailing a few months later.

Important Information to Give Your Destination Wedding Guests

○ The dates and the location. Be specific, and don't assume everyone will know where a city or resort is located. Give them the name of the country or island.

○ The hotel information, including how to make reservations and the rates of the rooms.

○ Recommendations of travel agents.

○ Information on getting around once they arrive. Include typical taxi fares and where to find them or rental car information.

○ A schedule of the weekend's activities with times and locations.

○ Information on the island, with typical weather conditions and dress code.

○ Any necessary travel requirements such as passports or visas and how to apply for them.

○ Details and contact information for resort activities that need to be prebooked.

○ Information for baby-sitting services.

It's a nice touch to include information on activities and baby-sitting, as well as the weekend schedule in each guest's room when they arrive. This way, they'll have the pertinent facts in case they forget to bring along the earlier mailing.

Destination Weddings

Do	Don't
✓ Think of your guests when selecting a destination.	✗ Neglect to ask about the rules for getting a marriage license at the destination.
✓ Visit your site ahead of time.	✗ Exclude guests from events.
✓ Send lots of details to your guests very early.	✗ Overschedule your guests.

19

You Mean There's More?

Even if you're not planning a destination wedding (see Chapter 18) but rather planning a wedding where you live, you can still plan other wedding-related parties. It's more and more common to include multiple events and planned activities for weddings, even if they take place in your hometown instead of on the other side of the globe. The options are really limitless, but in this chapter, I give you a breakdown of the most popular events and some tips to make them work.

The Last Hurrah!

I have to admit I've been known to roll my eyes when I hear the phrases *bachelor party* and *bachelorette party*. We've all heard the extreme tales of drunken revelry and embarrassment. I've even been lucky enough to try to get groomsmen down an aisle after an ill-timed bachelor party and can attest to the fact that people can actually look green.

These parties have become increasingly elaborate and involved in recent years, morphing from one night into a weekend or even a week away. I'm also thrilled to see that the parties have become more creative and less predictable. If you must have a final send-off, try to make it something you'll remember fondly and not something you hope will never be mentioned aloud again.

Bachelor Parties

It's the best man's job to plan and throw the bachelor party, along with the other groomsmen. He should take the groom's wishes into account (and if he is clever, the bride's) and plan a party where everyone will feel comfortable. He should also try to time the party to fit as many people's schedules as possible, although it may be impossible to accommodate everyone if many attendants are from out of town.

DON'T Wait Too Late

Having a bachelor party the night before the wedding is just asking for trouble. Plan this party well before the wedding so everyone can be rested and upright on the big day. Nothing ruins the look of a wedding more than ushers getting sick in the bushes in front of the church (and I speak from experience).

Instead of the traditional night of strip clubs and booze, many grooms are opting for something more interesting and less controversial. This ends up being more fun and keeps the bride happy (and prevents her from retaliating with her own wild night).

Creative Bachelor Party Alternatives

○ **A great dinner at a manly restaurant.** Think huge steaks, good wine, and fat cigars.

○ **An extreme weekend.** Athletic grooms may want a weekend of snowboarding, skydiving, or some other extreme sport.

○ **A golf tournament.** Transport all the guys to a golf resort for a few days.

- ○ **Camping out.** An outdoorsy groom may love a weekend hiking and camping with his buddies.

- ○ **Trip to a winery.** Get your guys together and spend a day tasting wines and eating well.

Bachelorette Parties

Once seen only rarely, bachelorette parties are becoming par for the course. They have come a long way from the bar crawls with the bride in a baseball cap complete with veil (thank God!) and now are more likely to be weekends for the bride to enjoy her girlfriends and some pampering. The maid or matron of honor usually plans the bachelorette party, with the other bridesmaids helping out.

Fun Options for Bachelorettes

- ○ **A slumber party.** Complete with palm readers and manicurists in attendance

- ○ **A weekend at a beach resort.** Think sun and water sports.

- ○ **A spa weekend.** A trip to a local day spa or even a short trip to a resort spa

- ○ **A trip to the city.** A jaunt to New York, Chicago, or another cool city for shopping, museums, and restaurants

- ○ **A ski weekend.** Envision a cozy lodge and hot toddies

Creative parties that celebrate your friendships will have many more lasting memories than drunken blurs. Think of the bride's favorite pastimes or hobbies, and make a weekend out of it. And a pitcher or two of margaritas wouldn't be a bad addition.

The Rehearsal Dinner

The rehearsal dinner is the most traditional of the wedding events because almost every wedding has one. The dinner can range in size from intimate gatherings of immediate family to huge receptions with almost every wedding guest in attendance. I've seen rehearsal dinners with bands, dancing, and even Teleprompters for the toasts!

Traditions and Trends

Usually held the night before the wedding, the rehearsal dinner is a time for the family and wedding party to get to know each other. It's the time for toasting and roasting, as well as for thanks from the bride and groom. This is the perfect time to give gifts to your attendants and to thank them for being a part of your celebration.

This dinner is usually hosted by the groom's family, but I have seen families split this expense or the bride's family assume the responsibility. As with most wedding expenses, the hard-and-fast rules are out the door. Do what works for your situation. If the groom's family can't host a huge formal dinner, have a much more informal gathering. A rehearsal dinner doesn't have to be formal to be loads of fun.

Rehearsal Dinner Trends

- **Picnics and cookouts.** These fun and casual events get everyone relaxed and in the mood for a fun wedding.

- **Dinner in a favorite neighborhood restaurant.** Consider serving Mexican, Italian, or sushi for this party.

- **Consider a dinner that isn't at dinner.** I've had clients do wonderful rehearsal lunches and brunches that don't keep folks up late the night before the wedding. I even have a client who is planning a delightful rehearsal breakfast with guests eating on picnic blankets outside!

○ **Cocktail parties with dancing.** Serve heavy hors d'oeuvres and have a band or DJ.

○ **Dinner at home.** Host the event in your home or a parent's or friend's home. Keep the numbers small for this intimate party.

DO **Consider Two Parties**

One of the biggest dilemmas brides have regarding the rehearsal dinner is the guest list. They want an intimate dinner, but they also want to include the out-of-town guests in the festivities. If having a rehearsal dinner nearly as large as your wedding is out of the question, consider having a small rehearsal dinner and then a dessert reception or cocktail party for the out-of-towners immediately following. This can be a fun way to include the guests who have traveled to your wedding in some type of pre-wedding party.

Rehearsal Dinner Mistakes to Avoid

Often brides and grooms don't put much thought into the rehearsal dinner. They book a restaurant, pick a menu, and forget about it until the evening arrives. It's better to think through the event as you would your wedding day. Plan the activities you'll have, and estimate the timing of the evening. If you'll have toasting, find out who plans to give a toast and appoint one person to start it off (usually the father of the groom) near the end of the meal after most of the clattering of plates and silverware has stopped. If you plan to show a video or have some other entertainment, be sure to plan when this will take place as well.

Rehearsal Dinner Goofs to Avoid

○ Don't make the rehearsal dinner so formal that it upstages the wedding.

○ Don't let the toasts drag on for so long that guests are exhausted the next day.

○ Don't serve the same food you'll be serving at the wedding. Two evenings of filet and salmon is too much, no matter how delicious.

○ Don't let guests get too intoxicated. You want folks bright-eyed and bushy-tailed for your wedding day.

○ Don't hold your dinner in the middle of a crowded restaurant and expect your toasts to be heard. Book a private room if you want guests to toast you. If it is a large room, consider a microphone.

○ Think about how your guests will get to the dinner, and consider providing transportation if the location is out of the way.

Thinking through your rehearsal dinner ahead of time will make the event go more smoothly and allow your guests to enjoy themselves. A short timeline for the event is helpful for the site as well as the main participants. This helps your toasters know when they'll be onstage and prevents the event from dragging out. Don't forget that the big event is still to come, so don't spend all your energy the night before.

Luncheons and Brunches

These events are not as common as the rehearsal dinner, but depending what area of the country you're from, you may be expected to host one. Hosting a luncheon for your bridesmaids or a farewell bunch for the out-of-town guests the day after the wedding is a lovely addition to the wedding weekend. These events are often more relaxed than the more formal events and are a time for people to enjoy themselves and not worry about any type of structure or format.

Let's Do Lunch

In some areas, tradition calls for the bride or her female relatives to host a luncheon for the bridesmaids. This can be on the wedding day (if time allows) or a day or two before the wedding. It's a gracious way for the bride to thank her bridesmaids and can be an appropriate time for her to give her attendants their gifts as well.

Bridesmaids luncheons can be held in a restaurant or in a private home and are usually kept to a small number. The mothers of the bride and groom and any close female relatives are usually included, but it may just be the bridesmaids and mothers.

Bye-Bye Brunch

Farewell brunches have risen in popularity as a way for couples to spend more time with their guests before they leave. Given the morning after the wedding, these parties are usually relaxed affairs where guests can come and go as their traveling schedules allow. You and your groom can either make an appearance or skip it and allow family and friends to mingle with each other.

Morning-after brunches can be held at a hotel where many guests are staying or at a private home nearby. Keep in mind that it will be much easier for guests to wander down from their rooms to a hotel brunch than it will be for them to trek out to a home. Brunches held at private homes usually draw a smaller crowd, which can be just fine. You certainly don't need to host another huge event after the wedding. Invitations to the brunch can be mailed separately (if you need a head count for the hotel), issued by phone, or just dropped into welcome bags for arriving guests.

Keeping Your Guests Busy

Another popular wedding trend is planning activities for the bridal party and guests outside the official wedding weekend parties. This is a way to keep people occupied and introduce them to your area's attractions.

It's a Girl Thing

The bridesmaids usually have a pretty busy schedule on the wedding day, but it's possible to squeeze in some fun and relaxation before the photos begin.

Wedding Day Activities for Bridesmaids

○ **Spa treatments.** If you aren't hosting a luncheon on the wedding day, consider pampering your girls with massages or manicures in the morning.

○ **Breakfast (almost) in bed.** Have breakfast sent to the salon or the hotel (if you hire the masseuses and manicurists to come to you) along with mimosas, and share a morning toast.

○ **A morning yoga or exercise class.** This can be a fun way to get your girls energized for the day and share time together.

○ **A sunrise run.** I even had a bride organize a charity running team for the Race for the Cure!

Amusing the Men

Traditionally, the groom and his attendants didn't have a thing to do on the wedding day except get themselves dressed and to the ceremony on time. Things have changed in recent years, as grooms have become more involved in the planning and have wanted to have as much fun as the girls.

208

You Mean There's More?

It's not uncommon for grooms to host a lunch for their attendants on the wedding day. This lunch can serve the same purpose as the bridesmaid's luncheon and can be a great time to thank the groomsmen and enjoy some relaxed moments before the madness ensues. Grooms can even get creative with wedding day activities.

Wedding Day Activities for Groomsmen

○ **A golf or tennis tournament.** Be sure to allow plenty of time!

○ **Groom the groomsmen.** Male-only salons are popping up in major cities and can be a fun way for guys to get masculine pampering while watching sports.

○ **A softball or volleyball game at a park.** Let them work out some of their nerves before the big event.

○ **A cookout.** Fire up the grill for a relaxed lunch at home.

Sad Story/Happy Ending

I always warn grooms to book an early tee time if they must play golf on their wedding day, and to wear lots of sunscreen. One groom forgot to do both and ended up arriving at the wedding completely harried because his game had run over and as red as a lobster! Luckily, the makeup artist was still on-site and was able to cover the sunburned groom with some concealer so he didn't look quite so fried. Don't forget the sunblock!

Because weddings have evolved into much more than just the ceremony and reception, it's important to plan the events surrounding your wedding. Think through how much you want to undertake, and be sure not to wedge too much into a few days. One or two nice events are always better than a slew of haphazard ones.

The Other Parties

Do	Don't
✓ Have a tasteful and creative bachelor/bachelorette party.	✗ Plan your last hurrah for the night before the wedding.
✓ Consider a reception after the rehearsal dinner for out-of-town guests.	✗ Let the rehearsal dinner upstage the wedding.
✓ Thank your attendants at the rehearsal dinner or bridesmaid's luncheon.	✗ Schedule too much on the wedding day.

20

After the Wedding

At several points during your wedding planning, you'll probably strongly suspect you should have eloped. When that feeling passes, you may start counting the days until the madness is over and you can get away from worries about bridesmaids' dresses, hors d'oeuvres, and finding the perfect favor.

When it all seems almost more than you can bear, remember: the honeymoon is your much-deserved reward after the marathon of planning. In this chapter, you learn how to plan a honeymoon that suits both you and your fiancé, plus get tips on how to tie up all the loose ends once you're back home.

The Great Escape

The honeymoon is a major part of your wedding planning and your budget, whether you include it in your overall budget and planning timeline or not. Be careful not to treat it as an afterthought to the wedding planning. It may very well be the most expensive trip you'll ever plan, so take the time to plan it as carefully as you plan your wedding day.

Finding the Perfect Getaway

Deciding on the perfect honeymoon destination is similar to looking for the ideal site for your wedding. You and your fiancé need to talk about what type of vacation you're looking for and then compromise to come up with a trip you will both enjoy. You may be a type A personality who isn't happy unless you have an itinerary of events every day, and your future husband may love nothing more than sitting on the beach. You have to find a happy medium by determining your honeymoon profile.

Determining Your Honeymoon Profile

○ Ask yourselves what your dream vacation would be if money and time were no object.

○ How much time do you both have to take off work?

○ What's your honeymoon budget?

○ What do you prefer to do when you travel?

○ What's your priority for your honeymoon: relaxing, sightseeing, trying new sports and activities, etc.?

○ What's the most important way to spend your honeymoon dollars: a luxurious hotel, first-class airfare, gourmet meals, an exotic and distant locale, activities, etc.?

DO Give Yourself a Break

Even if you're used to very active vacations and love the thought of spending hours wandering in museums, give yourself a little time to unwind after the wedding. Chances are you'll be exhausted, so don't be disappointed if you just don't have the energy or desire to play tourist right away. Give yourself a break, and allow yourself a few days of doing nothing before you venture out to hike up a volcano.

If your honeymoon profiles are completely at odds, don't despair. It isn't unusual to combine destinations to get the best of both worlds. You might relax for a few days on a beach before boarding a live-aboard ship for a few days of scuba diving. Be willing to be flexible. It's a vacation for both of you, after all!

After the Wedding

Legwork vs. Luxury

There are a few ways to go about planning your honeymoon (aside from dumping the job on your fiancé and letting him handle the whole mess). You can be industrious and do all the research on your own, or you can let a travel agent handle the bulk of the work. Be realistic about how much time and energy you have to devote to this project before you begin. If you decide to do the planning on your own, be ready to do lots of research.

Travel agents can be wonderful resources and can save you time and money in the long run. They also can give you the dirt on lots of vacation spots and resorts and where past couples have enjoyed the most. A good travel agent can work within your budget and tell you what is realistic as well. It's best to work with someone who plans lots of honeymoons instead of a corporate travel planner who may not be geared toward your needs. Talk to friends who have recently planned honeymoons, and get their feedback on their travel agents.

Items to Discuss with a Travel Agent

- Your budget.
- How much time you have for your trip.
- Your honeymoon profiles. This will help her match you to a destination.
- What type of room you'd like. Specify if you want a view, a private pool, or (heaven help us) a Jacuzzi shaped like a champagne glass.
- Whether you prefer all-inclusive resorts or traditional-style resorts and hotels.
- Whether you're interested in a cruise or a prepackaged tour.
- Any frequent flyer miles you have to use.

The more information you can give your travel agent, the better he or she can match you to your ideal vacation spot. If you've done any preliminary research into potential destinations, bring that information to share with your travel agent so he or she can get an idea of the types of venues that appeal to you.

DON'T Be Afraid to Ask

When you're interviewing potential travel agents, be sure to ask questions about how they prefer to work. It's important to know how accessible they will be and how to reach them in case of an emergency on your trip. Find out how helpful they will be in getting any special documents you'll need for your destination as well.

Surviving the Honeymoon

So you've booked the trip and have the tickets in hand. Now you have to prepare yourself for the trip and learn how to make the most of your budget while you're gone. Sure, you want this to be the trip of a lifetime, but there's no reason to waste your money in foolish areas just because you didn't know better.

Tips for Stretching Your Honeymoon Dollars

○ Cut back on the calls. Not that you'll want to be gabbing to your friends on the phone, but bring a cell phone or phone card if you must stay in touch.

○ Don't forget your toiletries. Get several travel sizes so you can throw them away and free up space in your luggage as you go.

○ Go off campus. Ask for recommendations of good local restaurants. Often the food is great and the prices are lower than the hotel restaurants.

○ Arrange your own activities and tours. Prepackaged activities are usually pricier.

○ Tell everyone from the airline desk clerk to the hotel concierge that you're on your honeymoon, and you may get upgrades and special amenities. Don't be annoying about it, though.

Sad Story/Happy Ending

One of my brides was notorious for doing everything at the last minute, which was bad for her and for my recurring eye twitch. Unfortunately, she didn't begin packing for her honeymoon to Italy until a couple days before the wedding, and when she went to get her passport, she couldn't find it. Of course this sent her off the deep end, and she and her fiancé turned their apartment upside down looking for it. Luckily, they found it tucked away in a drawer, but not without losing a few years off their lives because of the stress. Don't wait until the last minute to check your travel documents and get everything in order!

Don't leave honeymoon packing for the last minute. That's a surefire way to forget important items in all the wedding hustle-bustle. Make copies of the contents of your wallet, and put one copy in your luggage and leave one with a trusted friend. Then, if your purse is stolen, you'll have access to the information so you can quickly cancel your credit cards.

Checklist of Must-Pack Items

○ Passports that are valid for at least 6 months after the date of your trip. Don't wait until the last minute to take care of this!

○ Visas. Some countries require entry visas, which can take anywhere from a few days to more than a month to obtain. Start this process early as well.

○ Copies of all your travel documents, including your passport, visas, plane tickets, and hotel confirmations. Make several copies of your trip's itinerary.

○ Driver's licenses and a copy of your marriage license.

○ Your scuba diving certification (or C card) or sailing certification if you plan to go diving or rent a boat.

○ Medications and copies of all your prescriptions.

○ A copy of your eyeglass or contact prescription in case you lose yours and need to get an emergency replacement.

○ Camera, film, and extra batteries.

○ Your address book if you feel inclined to send postcards.

○ Electrical adaptors for foreign countries.

○ Sunscreen and bug repellant.

○ Plastic bags for wet bathing suits and sticky bottles of shampoo.

○ Aspirin, diarrhea medication, and antacid tablets.

○ Guidebooks and maps.

○ Books and magazines perfect for the beach.

○ Sunglasses.

Now that I've given you a huge list, I need to warn you not to overpack. Unless you're staying at a very fancy resort, bring one nice outfit (that packs easily) and lots of items that can be mixed and matched. Select fabrics that pack well so you won't look like a crumpled mess the entire trip. Ask for the dress code for your resort or ship so you can plan accordingly.

Is It Over Yet?

The honeymoon is over, and you're back from your blissful vacation. Then the cold, hard reality hits you. Your wedding is history, and now you need to go back to work and wrap up all the remaining details from your wedding. Although this can be a huge letdown, you can find comfort in the fact that you will soon have your wedding pictures and video to look at so you can relive the day a hundred times.

Tying Up Loose Ends

If you planned well, you should have very few loose ends to worry about once you get home from your honeymoon. The only bill that might be outstanding is the final costs of the catering and any services you extended on the wedding day. If you promised to send the band a check for playing an hour of overtime, don't forget to pop it in the mail as soon as you get home. Your wedding planner might send you a final invoice for any last-minute items she provided, such as amenity baskets for the ladies' rooms or welcome bags for the out-of-town guests.

If you have any questions about final bills or amounts charged to your credit cards, be sure to clear them up as soon as possible. Remember that you have been away for a few weeks already, so don't let outstanding bills or financial issues linger any longer than necessary.

Thanks for the Memories

I discussed the etiquette for sending thank you notes for your wedding gifts in Chapter 9. If you need a quick refresher, the rule is to write them as soon as possible. If you've been keeping up with gifts as they arrived, you shouldn't have an overwhelming stack. If you decided to let the thank yous pile up until after the wedding, you might be in a bit of trouble. The sooner you get started on them, the better.

After the wedding, it's nice to send thank you notes to the people who were involved in making your wedding a success. If your wedding ran pretty smoothly, you can bet a lot of people were working hard to make it appear seamless and easy. Wedding vendors are always thrilled to get thank you notes from clients. You'd be surprised at how many we never hear from again after months of daily contact! Take the time to write a short note to the people who made your wedding day come together, and you'll reserve your place in the bride hall of fame.

Sadly, we've come to the end of your wedding and the end of the book. Hopefully you've gotten some new ideas, learned what not to do when planning a wedding, and learned some insider tips to having a smooth and (mostly) stress-free wedding. Remember that attitude is everything when it comes to weddings. If you have fun with the planning and on the day, your happiness will spread to everyone around you and your wedding will be a huge success. So plan smart and enjoy yourself.

And if you *really* enjoy the planning process and suffer from major wedding planning withdrawal long after the honeymoon is over (if you're still buying wedding magazines 6 months later, I'm talking to you) and don't mind hanging around slightly neurotic (or sometimes very neurotic) brides all the time, maybe you should be a wedding planner, too. Just don't say I didn't warn you!

After the Wedding

Do	Don't
✓ Determine your honeymoon profile.	✗ Forget to plan time to relax and unwind during your honeymoon.
✓ Consider using a travel to plan your honeymoon.	✗ Leave your honeymoon agent packing until the last minute.
✓ Settle all your wedding bills and write thank you notes as soon as you return home.	✗ Forget to show your appreciation to your wedding vendors.

Glossary

aisle runner   A floor covering installed or rolled out over the ceremony aisle.

attrition clause   A clause in some hotel contracts that holds you responsible for a certain percentage of the estimated revenue.

banquet captain   The person responsible for all food service.

banquet event order (BEO)   A form prepared by an event facility providing detailed instructions on food and beverage and room setup.

base plate   A large empty plate in the center of each place setting that is removed before the entrée is served.

black tie   A term that indicates an event's required dress is a tuxedo for men and formal evening attire for women.

budget   A financial statement of estimated expenses.

buffet   A selection of food offered on a table; usually self-served.

cancellation clause   A provision in a contract that outlines penalties for cancellation of agreement.

capacity   The maximum number of people who can be accommodated in a space.

catering manager or **catering executive**   The person responsible for servicing food and beverage functions.

chair cover   A fabric cover used over a traditional chair. It can be stretched to fit the chair or tied on.

cocktail table   A small, round table between 15 and 30 inches in diameter used at receptions. The tall ones are called cabaret tables.

concierge   A hotel staff person who arranges services for guests, from reservations to tickets to tours.

consultant   A person who provides expert advice for a fee.

contract   A legal agreement between two or more persons that creates an obligation to perform a service with a penalty for failure to perform.

dance floor   An area for dancing; may be portable and assembled on-site.

deposit   A partial payment to secure a product or service. Security deposits may be returned if you leave things in one piece.

embossing   Impressed letters or artwork without ink.

engraving   The process of printing using an engraved metal plate.

estimate   Preliminary calculation of the cost of work to be done.

flat printing   A printing process that yields a flat surface.

floral designer   A specialist in designing with floral materials and décor.

font   A typeface style.

Force Majeure clause   A clause that limits liability if the event is prevented due to circumstances beyond control such as war, terrorism, strikes, or acts of God.

Glossary

French service   A method of banquet service in which each food item is served from a platter to an individual plate.

gobo   A light pattern projected onto a surface.

goodie bag   A bag for gifts given to guests.

gratuity   The amount paid as a reward for service. Also called the tip.

guarantee   In catering terms, the number of food and beverage servings to be paid for regardless of whether they are used or not.

guest list   A list of people's names invited to an event.

hors d'oeuvres   Appetizers.

inclusive   Rates that include tax and gratuity.

in-house services   Services provided by the venue, from catering to audiovisual.

itinerary   A detailed schedule of events.

Kettubah   The Jewish wedding contract usually signed before the ceremony.

kiddush cup   Ceremonial cups used for wine in Jewish ceremonies.

kosher   Food prepared according to Jewish dietary laws.

lavaliere microphone   A portable microphone that hooks to the speaker's clothing.

letterpress   A printing process that presses the ink into the paper.

linen   Tablecloths and napkins.

master of ceremonies (MC)   Person who makes introductions and announcements at an event.

minimum   The smallest amount to be served at an event. A surcharge may be added if the minimum revenue requirement is not met.

off-set printing   *See* flat printing.

off-site catering   Catering companies that travel to and work in various locales.

open bar   A full range of spirits paid for by the host; guests drink for free.

passport   A government document permitting travel to another country.

program   A schedule of events, sometimes listing participants, as in a wedding.

proposal   A plan detailing the offering and asking price. Or how the whole thing started in the first place.

raw footage   Total collection of videotape in an unedited format.

receiving line   The bride and groom and hosts (usually parents) lined up to greet guests after the wedding or at the reception.

registry   A service provided by many stores and websites in which people list selected merchandise for guests to access and purchase.

save-the-dates   Cards sent out well in advance of the wedding date to let guests know the date of the event. These are sent out even before the invitations.

shuttle service   Transportation for guests by coach or van from, for example, the wedding to the reception.

visa   An endorsement stamped in a tourist passport prior to entering a country.

white tie   Formal dress requiring white tie and tails for men and formal evening dress for women.

B

Resources

Here's the part you've been waiting for: lists of great wedding resources that will make your wedding planning and shopping a breeze! I've included sources I use all the time, as well as resources brides have found and passed along.

Websites

If you're like most brides I know (and me, I must confess), you love to get wedding information on the web. What better way to kill time at work and get great wedding ideas at the same time? In theory, you could plan and shop for your entire wedding without leaving your chair (although that can't be healthy!). Even if you prefer brick-and-mortar stores, the web is a great way to see your options before you venture out into the big wedding world. Just try not to get so sucked into the wedding web that you don't recognize your fiancé after a few weeks.

General Wedding Planning Sites

The Knot
www.theknot.com

The Wedding Channel
www.weddingchannel.com

Brides magazine
www.brides.com

Modern Bride magazine
www.modernbride.com

Grace Ormonde *Wedding Style*
www.weddingstylemagazine.com

Martha Stewart
www.marthastewart.com

Elegant Bride
www.elegantbride.com

"I Do" For Brides
www.idoforbrides.com

InStyle magazine
www.instyleweddings.com

Washington Weddings
www.dcwed.com

Maryland Weddings
www.marylandweddings.com

Two Brides
www.twobrides.com

Two Grooms
www.twogrooms.com

Industry Associations

International Special Events
Society
www.ises.com

Association of Bridal Consultants
www.bridalassn.com

Professional Photographers of
America
www.ppa.com

Wedding and Event Videographers
Association International
www.weva.com

Things to Wear

Dresses:

Simple Silhouettes
www.simpledress.com

Aria Bridesmaid
www.ariadress.com

Jenny Yoo Collection
www.jennyyoo.com

Siri
www.siriinc.com

Watters & Watters
www.watters.com

Priscilla of Boston
www.priscillaofboston.com

Nicole Miller
www.nicolemiller.com

BCBG Max Azria
www.bcbg.com

Lynn Lugo
www.lynnlugobridal.com

Accessories:

Bridal Gloves
www.bridalgloves.com

Turq Bridal
www.turqbridal.com

My Glass Slipper
www.myglassslipper.com

Grace Footwear
www.graziashoes.com

Headpieces by Toni
www.headpieces.com

Maria Elena Headpieces
www.mariaelenaheadpieces.com

Hair Comes the Bride
www.haircomesthebride.com

Little Blue Designs
www.littlebluedesigns.com

Beauty

Bridal Babe
www.bridalbabe.com

Bobbi Brown Cosmetics
www.bobbibrowncosmetics.com

Gustavo Cosmetics
www.gustavocosmetics.com

Wedding Favors and Fun Details

Bags and Bows
www.bagsandbowsonline.com

Beaucoup
www.beau-coup.com

Bella Regalo
www.bellaregalo.com

Wedding Things
www.weddingthings.com

Bella Terra
www.bellaterra.net

Sparklers Online
www.sparklersonline.com

Wedding Music Central
www.weddingmusiccentral.com

Wedding Favorites
www.weddingfavorites.com

My Wedding Labels
www.myweddinglabels.com

Bouquet Jewels
www.bouquetjewels.com

Papyrus
www.papyrusonline.com

Pamela's Parasols
www.pamelasparasols.com

Frills and Yummies
www.frillsandyummies.com

The Original Runner Company
www.OriginalRunner.com

Rentals and Linens

DC Rental
www.dcrental.com

Party Rental Ltd.
www.partyrentalltd.com

Unique Tabletop Rentals
www.uniquetabletoprentals.com

Ruth Fischl Linens
www.ruthfischl.com

Resource One
www.resourceone.info

Table Fashions, Ltd.
www.tablefashions.com

Resources

Invitations and Papers

You're Invited
www.youreinvited.com

Hannah Handmade Cards
www.hannahcards.com

Botanical Paperworks
www.botanicalpaperworks.com

The Calligraphy Lady
www.calligraphylady.com

Fine Stationery
www.finestationery.com

Mima Design
www.mimadesign.com

My Gatsby
www.mygatsby.com

Very Inviting
www.veryinviting.com

Mara Oatman Designs
www.maraoatmandesigns.com

Paper Mints
www.papermints.com

Design Envy
www.designenvy.com

Custom Programs
www.custom-programs.com

Registries

The Wedding List
www.theweddinglist.com

Pottery Barn
www.potterybarn.com

The Wedding Channel
www.weddingchannel.com

The Home Depot
www.homedepot.com

Tiffany and Company
www.tiffany.com

Target
www.target.com

Crate and Barrel
www.crateandbarrel.com

Bed, Bath and Beyond
www.bedbathandbeyond.com

Williams-Sonoma
www.williams-sonoma.com

Michael C. Fina
www.michaelcfina.com

Honeymoons and Travel

Travel agents and general travel sites:

Honeymoon Islands
www.honeymoonislands.com

McCabe Bremer Travel
www.mccabebremer.com

Honeymoons.com
www.honeymoons.com

Spa Finder
www.spafinder.com

Resorts and destinations:

Half Moon, Montego Bay, Jamaica
www.halfmoon.com.jm

Cap Juluca, Anguilla
www.capjuluca.com

The Ocean Club Paradise Island, Bahamas
www.oneandonlyresorts.com

Caneel Bay, St. John, U.S. Virgin Islands
www.caneelbay.com

SuperClubs Resorts
www.superclubs.com

Sandals Caribbean Resorts
www.sandals.com

Couples Resorts
www.couples.com

Lake Tahoe
www.tahoeweddingsites.com

Maui
www.visitmaui.com

Lanai
www.visitlanai.com

Hawaii's Big Island
www.bigisland.com

Oahu
www.visit-oahu.com

Turtle Island, Fiji
www.turtlefiji.com

Tahiti Legends
www.TahitiLegends.com

Windjammer Barefoot Cruises
www.windjammer.com

Relais and Châteaux
www.relaischateaux.fr

Hotel Katikies, Santorini, Greece
www.katikies.com

African Safari and Travel Inc.
www.go2africa.com

Cayman Islands
www.caymanislands.ky

Resources

Costas Careyes, Mexico
www.careyes.com.mx

Mexico Resorts
www.mexicoresorts.com

Maroma Resort and Spa, Riveria Maya, Mexico
www.maromahotel.com

Las Ventanas, Los Cabos, Mexico
www.lasventanas.com

For Further Reading

When you're eyes are bleary from surfing through wedding websites all day (or if, heaven forbid, you have to leave your computer), you can still get your wedding fix.

Magazines

Brides magazine
www.brides.com

Modern Bride magazine
www.modernbride.com

Martha Stewart Weddings
www.marthastewart.com

Grace Ormonde *Wedding Style*
www.weddingstylemagazine.com

Elegant Bride
www.elegantbride.com

InStyle Weddings
www.instyleweddings.com

"I Do" For Brides
www.idoforbrides.com

Engaged!
www.EngagedMagazine.com

Books

Cowie, Colin. *Weddings*. Boston: Little, Brown and Company, 1998.

Feinberg, Steven L. *Crane's Blue Book of Stationery*. New York: Simon & Schuster, 1993.

Post, Peggy. *Emily Post's Wedding Etiquette*. New York: HarperCollins Publishers, 2001.

Stewart, Martha. *The Best of Martha Stewart Living Weddings*. New York: Clarkson Potter Publishers, 1999.

Index

Index

Index

Index

menu cards, 168

message boards, 37-38

Modern Bride website, 34

month-by-month prioritized planning lists, 15

morning-after brunches, 207

museums, as reception sites, 51-52

music selection, 141
  bands, 143
    determining music style, 143-144
    questions to ask band, 145
    setting rules, 149-150
    test-driving, 144
    variety bands, 144
  cocktail music, 141
  dining music, 142
  DJs, 146-148

N–O

nonfloral décor, 122
  lighting, 123-125
  rentals, 122-123
  tent decor, 125

off-site caterers, 57-61

officiant selection, 151-152

offset printing, 81

online registries, 96

online shopping, 38-40

open-air trolleys (transportation option), 174

order of ceremony, 153-154

ordering
  invitations, 87-88
  wedding dress, 107

organization
  professional wedding planners, 17-18
    qualifications, 18-20
    selection process, 20-22
  timelines, 11
    deadlines, 13-16
    fluidity, 16-17
    generic lists, 11
    setting priorities, 12-13

Original Runner Co. website, 39

outdoor weddings, 45-46, 54-55

P

packing for the honeymoon, 215-216

parties (wedding-related parties), 201-209
  bachelor parties, 202-203
  bachelorette parties, 203
  luncheons and brunches, 206-207
  rehearsal dinners, 204-206
  wedding day activities for bridesmaids, 208
  wedding day activities for groomsmen, 208-209

permits, 183

personal appearance, 112-114

personal wedding style, 6-8

personal wedding websites, 40-42

Q–R

qualifications (wedding planners), 18-20

receiving lines, 186
reception sites, 46-47
  at-home weddings, 53-54
  garden weddings, 54-55
  historic homes and mansions, 52-53
  hotels, 48-49
  museums, 51-52
  private clubs, 49
  selection process, 47-48
  ships and boats, 55-56
  wedding halls, 50-51
registry (gifts), 93-97
  alternatives, 95
  appointments, 95
  choosing places to register, 94
  discretion, 97
  online registries, 96
  questions to ask yourself, 93-94
  thank you notes, 97
rehearsals, coordination, 184-185
religion
  blending religions, 156-157
  religious sites, 43-45
rentals, nonfloral decor, 122-123
research
  honeymoon, 213
  Internet, 33
   group sites, 36
   mega-site browsing tips, 34-35

   message boards, 37-38
   online shopping, 38-40
   personal wedding websites, 40-42
   surfing wedding websites, 33-34
   vendor sites, 36
resources, honeymoon information, 213
restroom amenities, 170
room-block contracts (hotels), 75-76

S

save-the-date cards, 81-82
schedule
  destination weddings, 198
  wedding coordination, 186-188
seamstresses, 105
seasonal flowers, 119
setting limits, guest lists, 69-71
setting the wedding date, 2
shipboard weddings, 55-56
shopping
  bridesmaids' dresses, 108-111
  groomsmen attire, 111
  online, 38-40
  wedding dress, 103-107
showers (bridal showers), 98-100
shuttle buses (transportation option), 174
sites
  ceremony sites, 43-46
  destination weddings, 197-198